STACKS

INTRODUCING
ISSUES WITH
OPPOSING
VIEWPOINTS®

Sexually Transmitted Diseases

David Haugen, Susan Musser, and
Michael Chaney, *Book Editors*

GREENHAVEN PRESS
A part of Gale, Cengage Learning

GALE
CENGAGE Learning·

Farmington Hills, Mich • San Francisco • New York • Waterville, Maine
Meriden, Conn • Mason, Ohio • Chicago

Elizabeth Des Chenes, *Director, Content Strategy*
Douglas Dentino, *Manager, New Product*

For more information, contact:
Greenhaven Press
27500 Drake Rd.
Farmington Hills, MI 48331-3535
Or you can visit our Internet site at gale.cengage.com

For product information and technology assistance, contact us at

Gale Customer Support, 1-800-877-4253
For permission to use material from this text or product, submit all requests online at
www.cengage.com/permissions

Further permissions questions can be e-mailed to permissionrequest@cengage.com

Articles in Greenhaven Press anthologies are often edited for length to meet page requirements. In addition, original titles of these works are changed to clearly present the main thesis and to explicitly indicate the author's opinion. Every effort is made to ensure that Greenhaven Press accurately reflects the original intent of the authors. Every effort has been made to trace the owners of copyrighted material.

LIBRARY OF CONGRESS CATALOGING-IN-PUBLICATION DATA

Sexually transmitted diseases / David Haugen, Susan Musser, and Michael Chaney, book editors.
     pages cm -- (Introducing issues with opposing viewpoints)
   Summary: "This title explores many aspects of sexually transmitted diseases, including what contributes to the spread of sexually transmitted diseases, what education programs address the spread of STDs, and whether government regulation would reduce STD infection rates"-- Provided by publisher.
  Includes bibliographical references and index.
  ISBN 978-0-7377-6928-9 (hardback)
  1. Sexually transmitted diseases. 2. Sexual health. I. Haugen, David M., 1969- editor of compilation. II. Musser, Susan, editor of compilation. III. Chaney, Michael, 1949- editor of compilation.
  RC200.2.S4816 2014
  616.95'1--dc23
                                                              2014000752

Printed in the United States of America
1 2 3 4 5 6 7 18 17 16 15 14

Contents

Foreword

I ndulging in a wide spectrum of ideas, beliefs, and perspectives is a critical cornerstone of democracy. After all, it is often debates over differences of opinion, such as whether to legalize abortion, how to treat prisoners, or when to enact the death penalty, that shape our society and drive it forward. Such diversity of thought is frequently regarded as the hallmark of a healthy and civilized culture. As the Reverend Clifford Schutjer of the First Congregational Church in Mansfield, Ohio, declared in a 2001 sermon, "Surrounding oneself with only like-minded people, restricting what we listen to or read only to what we find agreeable is irresponsible. Refusing to entertain doubts once we make up our minds is a subtle but deadly form of arrogance." With this advice in mind, Introducing Issues with Opposing Viewpoints books aim to open readers' minds to the critically divergent views that comprise our world's most important debates.

Introducing Issues with Opposing Viewpoints simplifies for students the enormous and often overwhelming mass of material now available via print and electronic media. Collected in every volume is an array of opinions that captures the essence of a particular controversy or topic. Introducing Issues with Opposing Viewpoints books embody the spirit of nineteenth-century journalist Charles A. Dana's axiom: "Fight for your opinions, but do not believe that they contain the whole truth, or the only truth." Absorbing such contrasting opinions teaches students to analyze the strength of an argument and compare it to its opposition. From this process readers can inform and strengthen their own opinions, or be exposed to new information that will change their minds. Introducing Issues with Opposing Viewpoints is a mosaic of different voices. The authors are statesmen, pundits, academics, journalists, corporations, and ordinary people who have felt compelled to share their experiences and ideas in a public forum. Their words have been collected from newspapers, journals, books, speeches, interviews, and the Internet, the fastest growing body of opinionated material in the world.

Introducing Issues with Opposing Viewpoints shares many of the well-known features of its critically acclaimed parent series, Opposing Viewpoints. The articles are presented in a pro/con format, allowing readers to absorb divergent perspectives side by side. Active reading questions preface each viewpoint, requiring the student to approach the material thoughtfully and carefully. Useful charts, graphs, and cartoons supplement each article. A thorough introduction provides readers with crucial background on an issue. An annotated bibliography points the reader toward articles, books, and websites that contain additional information on the topic. An appendix of organizations to contact contains a wide variety of charities, nonprofit organizations, political groups, and private enterprises that each hold a position on the issue at hand. Finally, a comprehensive index allows readers to locate content quickly and efficiently.

Introducing Issues with Opposing Viewpoints is also significantly different from Opposing Viewpoints. As the series title implies, its presentation will help introduce students to the concept of opposing viewpoints and learn to use this material to aid in critical writing and debate. The series' four-color, accessible format makes the books attractive and inviting to readers of all levels. In addition, each viewpoint has been carefully edited to maximize a reader's understanding of the content. Short but thorough viewpoints capture the essence of an argument. A substantial, thought-provoking essay question placed at the end of each viewpoint asks the student to further investigate the issues raised in the viewpoint, compare and contrast two authors' arguments, or consider how one might go about forming an opinion on the topic at hand. Each viewpoint contains sidebars that include at-a-glance information and handy statistics. A Facts About section located in the back of the book further supplies students with relevant facts and figures.

Following in the tradition of the Opposing Viewpoints series, Greenhaven Press continues to provide readers with invaluable exposure to the controversial issues that shape our world. As John Stuart Mill once wrote: "The only way in which a human being can make some approach to knowing the whole of a subject is by hearing what can be said about it by persons of every variety of opinion and studying all modes in which it can be looked at by every character of mind. No wise man ever acquired his wisdom in any mode but this." It is to this principle that Introducing Issues with Opposing Viewpoints books are dedicated.

Introduction

*"STDs are hidden epidemics of enormous health and economic conse-
quence in the United States. They are hidden because many Americans are
reluctant to address sexual health issues in an open way and because of the
biologic and social characteristics of these diseases. All Americans have an
interest in STD prevention because all communities are impacted by STDs
and all individuals directly or indirectly pay for the costs of these diseases."*

—Centers for Disease Control and Prevention, foreword
to *Sexually Transmitted Disease Surveillance 2011*

Sexually transmitted diseases, or STDs, have plagued humanity
from ancient times. For much of recorded history, the pathogens that caused these diseases could not be counteracted. Early
medical science could offer no cures, allowing infections to wreak
havoc in populations that had no protections against their spread. An
epidemic of syphilis, for example, spread throughout Europe in the
late fifteenth century, leaving millions sickened or dead in its wake.
Until doctors began seriously studying these diseases and finding remedies, confusion clouded diagnosis and treatment. Up until the eigh-
teenth century, for example, most medical professionals assumed that
there was only one kind of sexually transmitted infection—an ailment
they simply labeled "venereal disease"; however, diligent research and
innovations in microbiology led physicians to discover the agents
responsible for individual diseases. Identification and chemical treatments eventually arrested the wide-scale devastation brought about
by outbreaks of these infections.

By the 1960s and 1970s the prevalence of antibiotics and public
health campaigns helped bring many STDs under control. For some
sufferers, medicine provided cures or at least control of the effects.
For the broader population, though, information on these diseases
made people aware of the risks and dangers as well as the course of
action to take in response to contracting one. While once sexually
transmitted diseases were conceived as a mark of personal shame and
irresponsibility, modern medicine characterizes them as public health

threats that require immediate response and broad countermeasures. Today, there are over two dozen sexually transmitted viruses, bacteria, and parasites known to plague humanity.

As the name makes plain, sexually transmitted diseases are any of a host of infections spread through sexual contact of any kind. It is the moist mucous membranes present on the body parts engaged in these sexual acts that allow the pathogens to transfer between individuals. While, indeed, sexual transmission is the most common, STDs can also be conveyed through the blood: from mother to fetus, from donor to recipient of transfusions, or from one drug user to another who share a hypodermic needle. Babies may also acquire certain STDs through breast-feeding. Because it is possible to contract these infections from people who appear healthy and may be unaware of being infected, some professionals prefer to use the term *sexually transmitted infection* (STI) instead of *sexually transmitted disease*. When the HIV/AIDS epidemic surfaced in the 1980s, physicians favored the use of *STI* because many carriers of the human immunodeficiency virus (HIV) showed no symptoms of the acquired immunodeficiency syndrome (AIDS) yet could easily pass on the pathogen and cause the full-blown disease in the recipient. Regardless, of whether the carrier exhibits the symptoms of the disease, the methods of infection remain the same.

The infection routes provide the means for each type of STD pathogen to spread. Viral pathogens such as hepatitis B, herpes simplex, molluscum contagiosum, and human papillomavirus (HPV) are conveyed through body fluids or through skin/mucous membrane contact. Bacteria pathogens that cause syphilis, chlamydia, gonorrhea, chancroids, and granuloma inguinale follow the same paths. Candidiasis (commonly referred to as a yeast infection) is a fungus that also passes through skin and mucous membranes. Trichomoniasis is the result of a protozoan parasite transmitted during intercourse. Scabies are minute mites and lice are tiny insects that infest hosts via contact with skin or pubic hair. The symptoms of each infection vary. Scabies and lice cause an itching, some bacterial infections cause painful burning in the genital region, herpes manifests in blisters, and HIV can seriously compromise an individual's immune system. Some, such as herpes, HIV, and HPV can lead to cancers and death.

Many STDs can be treated and cured. Herpes and HIV, however, still have no known cures. The prevalence of herpes is decreasing in the US population. The Centers for Disease Control and Prevention (CDC) concludes that in the late 1980s to mid-1990s, herpes simplex virus was reported in 21 percent of Americans visiting their doctors; in 2008 the number was down to 16.2 percent (though nearly 19 percent of those individuals are unaware that they carry the infection). Reported HIV cases are on the rise in the United States, though the rate of infection is stable. The CDC notes that about 3 percent of the population is infected with HIV (though again, over 18 percent of those persons are unaware of their infection). Because these diseases can be ravaging if left undiagnosed and untreated, health officials have focused efforts on prevention to curb outbreaks.

Since the early 1980s when HIV/AIDS garnered media attention in the United States, health organizations, politicians, and media personalities have spoken out in favor of various ways to increase protection against sexually transmitted diseases. Abstinence, monogamy, and correct use of prophylactics such as condoms are still touted by different groups with different agendas to halt what became a tragic epidemic. The competing methods centered controversy on the medical and moral issues surrounding the disease. Some believe that herbal remedies are more worthwhile than antiretroviral drugs typically prescribed as therapy. More recently, the drug company Gilead has put its faith in marketing Truvada, a once-a-day pill that prevents infection in uninfected individuals. Gilead's critics argue that marketing such a pill will encourage unsafe sex. According to a January 1, 2012, article for *Belle News,* Michael Weinstein, president of the Los Angeles AIDS Healthcare Foundation, asserted, "I believe that this could be catastrophic in terms of HIV prevention." He and others like him fear such preventive measures will lead to a rise in STDs across the board. Proponents of the pill insist that fighting the spread of the disease should justify the pill's use.

On the moral front, religious groups have been notably vocal on the means of preventing the spread of HIV and other STDs. The Catholic Church, for instance, contends that condom use is not the right response to HIV infection. Not alone in this among Christian denominations, the Catholic Church maintains that teaching abstinence is a more significant yet underused tool. "When educating on the great questions of affectivity [emotions] and sexuality," Pope Benedict XVI stated in 2010, "we must avoid showing adolescents and young people ways that tend to devalue these fundamental dimensions of human existence." To the church, providing prophylactic education in schools or in the media often endorses (even if unintentionally) the message that promiscuity is tolerable and that chastity is unrealistic. Kathleen Dwyer, writing for Virginia Tech's student newspaper, the *Collegiate Times*, penned an opinion piece that rejected abstinence-only education on the grounds that young people have never and will never refrain from sexual experimentation. "School-age children are still becoming sexually involved, but because of abstinence-only education, they lack proper information regarding their health and safety," Dwyer claims. She and other critics maintain that abstinence may be the right choice for some, but it is unrealistic to suppose that STDs or pregnancies can be stopped by working under the hope that all young people will faithfully adhere to no-sex-before-marriage exhortations.

The discussion concerning the prescribing of prophylactics to young people is only one of the debates that surround the recognition of and response to sexually transmitted diseases. In *Introducing Issues with Opposing Viewpoints: Sexually Transmitted Diseases*, several medical professionals and other experts give their opinion on these matters. Some examine possible means to combat the spread of STDs; others debate whether these means are practical and ethical. All hope that contemporary society can curb these pernicious infections, but, as this anthology demonstrates, the paths toward prevention are still a subject of controversy.

Chapter 1

What Contributes to the Spread of Sexually Transmitted Diseases?

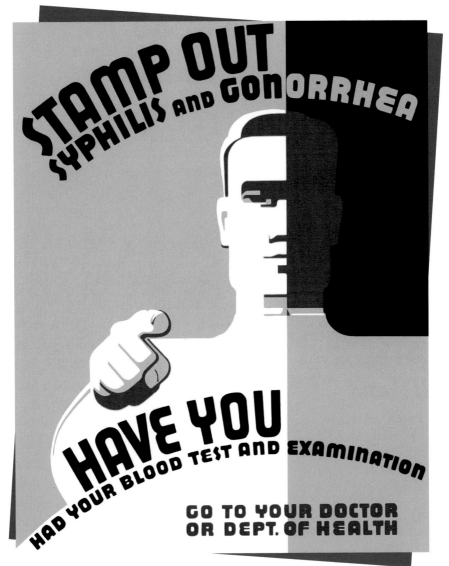

An early prevention poster urges people to be tested for sexually transmitted diseases.

Lack of AIDS Awareness in the Gay Community Has Led to Increases in Infection Rates

"Today . . . we're so caught up in the giddiness of the marriage-equality movement that we've abandoned the collective fight against HIV and AIDS."

Peter Staley

In the viewpoint that follows AIDS and gay rights activist Peter Staley contends that the increased rates of HIV and AIDS infections in the gay community have resulted from gay rights groups' shift in focus away from the disease and toward civil rights issues. While Staley credits the gay rights movement of the eighties and nineties with successfully reducing the rates of HIV and AIDS in the gay community and understands the shift in focus to a happier topic, he implores these activists to remember that the struggle against the disease continues and warrants attention. He asserts that with the Supreme Court ruling striking down the Defense of Marriage Act, this shift in resources back to AIDS can occur without losing ground in the fight for marriage equality and that the gay community can maintain the sense of broader love and purpose that previously helped them to begin to win the battle against AIDS.

AS YOU READ, CONSIDER THE FOLLOWING QUESTIONS:

1. According to statistics from the CDC cited by Staley, by how much did HIV infection rates increase in young gay men from 2008 to 2010?
2. What does the author state to be the difference in ACT UP New York's budget for AIDS today as compared with the early 1990s?
3. By how much did Massachusetts HIV infection rates drop from 2000 to 2009 after Medicaid was expanded to include people with HIV, according to the author?

Same-sex love, once "the love that dare not speak its name," has been affirmed by the highest court in the land. With its decision in *Windsor* [*v. United States*], the Supreme Court established that the federal government cannot deny the "personhood and dignity" of legally married same-sex couples. It's a stunning turnaround for a court that 27 years ago said gay sex was not entitled to legal protections, even behind closed doors. It's a moment gay rights advocates deserve to celebrate.

But in our exaltation over wedded bliss, we are forgetting another kind of "til death do us part": the bonds that tie us together as a group, across social strata, race and generations—the same bonds that helped us fight AIDS.

During the worst years of the AIDS crisis, from 1981 to the advent of effective medications in 1996, the gay community forged a new definition of love: It encompassed traditional romantic love, but it went beyond the love between two people. Often shunned by our biological families, we created our own, complete with brothers and sisters who cared and fought for one another and elders who mentored the young. You only had to be at the 1987 meeting when ACT UP [AIDS Coalition to Unleash Power] was formed—as the 52-year-old playwright Larry Kramer looked down on a packed hall of people half his age, exhorting us to fight for our lives—to know that we were about to embark on a remarkable journey together.

Today, though, we're so caught up in the giddiness of the marriage-equality movement that we've abandoned the collective fight against HIV and AIDS.

HIV and AIDS Remain a Serious Problem in the Gay Community

And yes, it's still a fight. HIV remains the largest health issue facing the gay community. From 2008 to 2010, according to the Centers for Disease Control and Prevention (CDC), new HIV infections remained steady overall but rose a startling 22 percent in young gay men. At the current rates, more than half of college-aged gay men will become HIV-positive by the age of 50.

The fact that effective HIV treatment now exists doesn't resolve the problem. In 2012, the CDC reported that of the more than 1 million Americans infected with HIV, only 25 percent were able to access and adhere to treatment. Nearly 6,000 gay men with AIDS die each year in the United States. Moreover, even well-treated HIV demands a lifetime of daily medication. Between that burden and the social stigma that unfortunately accompanies an HIV diagnosis, living with this disease can be difficult.

Gay Marriage Has Become the Top Issue for Gay Rights Groups

Yet these community health concerns have been eclipsed by advocacy and fundraising around marriage. The nation's largest gay rights groups do almost no programmatic work on HIV/AIDS. The words "HIV" and "AIDS" don't even appear in the most recent annual

Nearly six thousand gay men in the United States die each year from AIDS. A lack of awareness about AIDS has been cited as a contributive factor.

reports from the big three: the Human Rights Campaign (HRC), the Gay and Lesbian Alliance Against Defamation (GLAAD) and the National Gay and Lesbian Task Force (NGLTF). By contrast, the Cornell University Library's collection includes 23 boxes of NGLTF documents from the 1980s and '90s outlining the group's AIDS work.

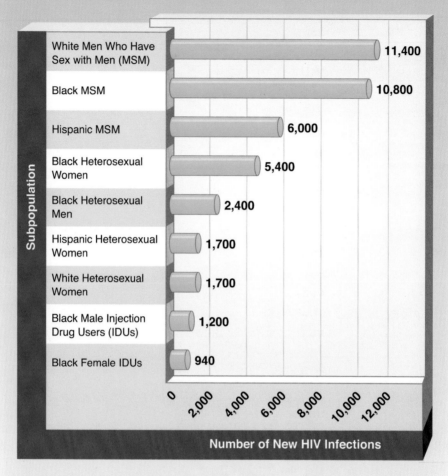

Estimates of New HIV Infections by Race/Ethnicity, Sexual Orientation, and Gender in 2009

Subpopulation	Number of New HIV Infections
White Men Who Have Sex with Men (MSM)	11,400
Black MSM	10,800
Hispanic MSM	6,000
Black Heterosexual Women	5,400
Black Heterosexual Men	2,400
Hispanic Heterosexual Women	1,700
White Heterosexual Women	1,700
Black Male Injection Drug Users (IDUs)	1,200
Black Female IDUs	940

Taken from: Centers for Disease Control and Prevention. "New HIV Infections in the United States," December 2012.

"HIV/AIDS policy was the gay movement's top priority then, and we fought it on multiple fronts," said Urvashi Vaid, the NGLTF's executive director from 1989 to 1992 and then again in the late '90s. "There is no denying that HIV issues have been less a focus of the LGBT [lesbian, gay, bisexual, and transgender] movement."

Groups that remain dedicated to HIV/AIDS have struggled to attract contributions. In the early 1990s, ACT UP New York's budget was more than $1 million a year, but it now fights AIDS with a budget of less than $20,000. Meanwhile, HRC, having thrown its full weight behind the marriage push, operates with a budget of more than $45 million.

The Fight Against AIDS Was Emotionally Draining

In some ways, the shift in attention is understandable. Causing untold sickness and death, AIDS consumed gay activism from the early 1980s to the mid-1990s. By the time effective antivirals started bringing down the death rates, we were all so emotionally spent by the plague years that many of us wanted to believe that our job there was finished.

I was no exception. I'd been an AIDS activist since shortly after my HIV diagnosis in 1985 at the age of 24. In my mid-30s, I wanted to get as far away from AIDS as I could. Many of my friends had died, and as a survivor, I struggled to adjust to a future I never thought I'd have. I was eventually drawn back to activism by evidence of rising rates of infection. But I can understand why many gay activists and their allies pivoted—and never turned back.

After all, who wants to relive sadness while a happy story is in progress? Same-sex marriage is about love, acceptance and, recently, a stream of political victories, while AIDS is one of the biggest downers of our time.

I have to wonder if race plays a role, too. Is there more empathy within the white gay community for the (mostly white) gay couples we see on TV seeking marriage equality than there is for the young, gay black men who account for many of the new HIV infections?

Gay Organizations Can Still Make a Difference in Fighting HIV and AIDS

Now, as the leading gay organizations and foundations regroup after the successes at the Supreme Court, it's time to find our voice again against HIV and AIDS.

I'm not saying we should let up on same-sex marriage. It's a worthy cause. I hardly imagined that I'd live to see the day when my partner of 19 years and I might enjoy not only the full rights and privileges of married straight couples but the incredible sense of social affirmation and inclusion that comes with that. Yet with gay marriage legal in only 12 states and the District of Columbia, the fight is far from over.

Given the strength of the marriage movement, though, surely the major gay rights organizations could reappropriate just 10 percent of their budgets to fighting HIV and AIDS.

Contrary to the prevailing skepticism, that battle is not a lost cause. Treating people with antivirals both keeps them alive and prevents them from infecting others. Massachusetts saw its HIV infection rates drop 45 percent between 2000 and 2009, largely because it expanded Medicaid to include people with HIV, not just AIDS; because its universal health-care system got more people onto treatment regimens; and because it launched targeted testing, prevention and treatment programs. With Obamacare [the Affordable Care Act], we have the potential to replicate those gains nationally, but only if there's a concerted push.

On Wednesday morning [June 28, 2013], when the Supreme Court released its gay-marriage opinions, I was attending an HIV working group session at a hotel off Dupont Circle [in Washington, DC]. We took a break to follow the coverage on SCOTUSblog [Supreme Court of the United States blog]: cheering for the majority opinions, cringing at Justice Antonin Scalia's dissent. And then it was back to work.

As we continue to see gay love enshrined in law, we shouldn't forget the broader form of love—of our entire community—that has sustained us and brought us this far.

EVALUATING THE AUTHOR'S ARGUMENTS:

After reading Peter Staley's analysis of the change in gay rights groups' focus from HIV and AIDS to marriage equality, do you think the shift was appropriate considering the success of the push in the 1990s and the emotional toll this activism took on activists? Should the gay community refocus its efforts on AIDS, as Staley suggests? Why or why not?

The Men Who Want AIDS— And How It Improved Their Lives

"It's not just those who already have AIDS who view it as a lifeline; some young men who test negative aspire to contract the disease as a way out of trouble."

Maral Noshad Sharifi

As HIV and AIDS infection rates in the gay community have continued to increase in recent years, gay rights activists and members of the community have rededicated efforts to investigate why and how to halt the increase, reports Maral Noshad Sharifi in the following viewpoint. Sharifi, one of her interviewees with AIDS, and individuals who work for a range of social services groups all suggest that for homeless people living in New York, particularly gay men, becoming infected with HIV presents an opportunity to obtain rent assistance, food stamps, and health care, among other services. Additionally, according to the author, this assistance can only be acquired when the condition worsens to dangerous levels, thus encouraging individuals to abstain from taking their medication. The author and the experts cited in the viewpoint suggest that provision of social services prior to homelessness or infection would help to alleviate the problem. Sharifi is a freelance journalist and documentary filmmaker.

AS YOU READ, CONSIDER THE FOLLOWING QUESTIONS:

1. When did James Bolas, director of a nonprofit in New York, first become aware of homeless people intentionally contracting AIDS to become eligible for benefits?
2. As of May 2013, how many people was HASA serving and how many were under the age of eighteen, according to the author?
3. What does Sage Rivera, as cited by Sharifi, believe could be done to prevent HIV infections in the individuals who are grateful to have the disease?

'Don't take no meds, don't go to a doctor. And that's what I did. I sabotaged myself to get my numbers down.'

Tye Fortner has fine, delicate ears, a newly pierced eyebrow, and a trim beard. He's wearing honey-colored contact lenses and a Jimi Hendrix T-shirt. "I wanted to be presentable," he explains as a photographer snaps his portrait. "I was going to buy an outfit, but it was so hot."

We are standing outside his apartment block in the Fordham area of the Bronx in New York City on a muggy Friday afternoon in June, a few days before Pride. A woman walks by pushing a wheeled cart from which she's selling Italian ices. "Hey mama!" Fortner calls to her and asks for a scoop of mango and cherry that stains his teeth red. Refreshed, he leads the way up the stairs to the roof of his building, where he takes out a packet of Newports and, perched high above the city, begins to tell his story.

Fortner was 22 and homeless when he started feeling weak, with crushing stomach pain and terrible headaches. A sex worker from the age of 16, sometimes too high on crack to remember to use protection, he had been putting off the inevitable for weeks before he finally decided to get tested for HIV. The result came back positive.

"My whole world changed," Fortner says, recalling the moment six years ago when he received his diagnosis. At first it changed for the worse as he struggled to come to terms with his diagnosis.

But then, it changed for the better.

After years of homelessness and a day-to-day existence, Fortner, now 28, was faced with the tantalizing prospect of a place to sleep, regular meals, and more thorough New York City services provided to people who reach a certain stage of the disease. First he would have to meet their diagnosis requirements; then he would receive help.

"I didn't know about the services," he says. "I didn't know that once you have AIDS you're entitled to all this other stuff."

That silver lining was a surprise to Fortner. And while it might seem counterintuitive, contracting the virus has made life easier for other young homeless men in New York City, who in return for developing full-blown AIDS gain a roof over their heads and basic services.

This cruel paradox—having to get really sick in order to enjoy a better, more comfortable life—has not gone unnoticed. "I have experienced people [who are] grateful that they have HIV," says Sage Rivera, a research associate at the Centers for Disease Control and Prevention who has worked with hundreds of LGBT youth. "It's sort of like a sigh of relief or an extra boost," he says. "There are a whole bunch of different names for HIV within the [LGBT] community: 'the monster,' 'the kitty,' 'the scratch,' 'the gift that keeps on giving.' So people say, 'I have the kitty—so now I can get my place. Now I can get hooked up; I can get my food stamps, I can get this, I can get that.'

"Other people say, 'I do not know what I would have done without the monster.' I can think of five boys, automatically, who've told me this."

And it's not just those who already have AIDS who view it as a lifeline; some young men who test negative aspire to contract the disease as a way out of trouble. Rivera knows at least one man who planned to have unprotected sex on purpose, an attitude he sums up thus: "My life is not getting better. I need a helping hand, and it seems like the only way I can get a helping hand is by getting sick."

For Fortner, the phenomenon of young men deliberately contracting HIV is dispiriting but not surprising. "When you're on the streets every day—winter, summer, spring, and fall—and you find a way to have an apartment of your own, it looks better," he says. His own experience is instructive: Once his AIDS was diagnosed, he was astonished at how much easier it was to live in New York City. "Right now the rent for my apartment is $1,150, but because I'm on the program

I only pay $217, which leaves me with about $400 a month," he says. "That's still a struggle, but I feel gifted, because one way or another I pull through."

Pulling through by contracting HIV is the kind of specter that alarms people like James Bolas, director of education for the nonprofit Empire State Coalition in New York. "It's sad that really young people are forced to take this measure in order to survive," he says, adding that he first heard about young homeless people rationalizing HIV infection as a means to obtain benefits as early as 1987, when the virus was still untreatable.

Nancy Downing, director of advocacy and legal services at Covenant House New York, a youth shelter, has also learned of kids who consider getting infected with HIV/AIDS as a means of survival. "It's bone-crushing," she says. "It's unbelievable that kids have to go those lengths to get the services they need. Young people are sometimes not looking at their long-term future—they can see only the short-term future—and that is a developmental issue. It's going to have an impact on them for the rest of their lives. Some might not even take the medication, because at their age—again, developmentally—they might not see the need."

Despite the wealth of anecdotal evidence, the New York State Office of Children and Family Services, through its Office of Youth Development—which helps oversee and fund programs for homeless youth—says it is unaware of homeless gay youth purposely getting infected with HIV/AIDS as a way to obtain services. Meanwhile, the New York City Department of Youth and Community Development, responsible for providing homeless youth in New York City with the services and resources they need to stabilize their lives, would give no comment.

To be eligible for the services provided by New York City's HIV/AIDS Services Administration, commonly referred to as HASA, people must be diagnosed with AIDS or have HIV with certain other specified medical conditions, says Dr. Robert Grossberg, medical director of the Montefiore AIDS clinic in the Bronx. Those eligible for HASA services get a living plan, housing assistance, financial aid, and free medical care. Exactly what each person gets is determined on a case-by-case basis, depending on factors like their income level.

Estimated New HIV Infections Among Men Who Have Sex with Men Aged Thirteen to Twenty-Four, 2008–2010

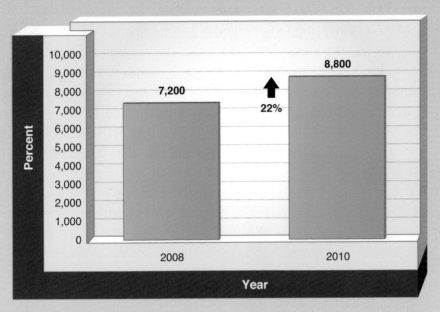

Taken from: Centers for Disease Control and Prevention. "New HIV Infections in the United States," December 2012.

The housing assistance consists of immediate temporary placement in an SRO (single room occupancy) building, which has individual and two-person rooms with shared kitchens and bathrooms, until a permanent apartment is found. Once a permanent apartment is found, HASA covers the rent but residents pay for their own utilities, such as electricity and gas.

In May 2013, HASA was serving 43,845 people, of whom 65.3% were adult men; it also served 156 youth aged 17 and younger. The Bronx has the highest HASA representation of the boroughs, at 36.7%, followed by Brooklyn, Manhattan, Queens, and Staten Island, respectively. Half of those eligible for services are African American, one-third are Latino, and just fewer than 9% are white.

We leave Fortner's rooftop and retire to O'Brien's, an Irish pub a few blocks away. Most of the barstools are occupied by middle-aged Irish Americans watching golf. There are portraits of racehorses on the walls alongside illustrated maps of "Lovely Leitrim," a mountainous county in Ireland. Behind the bar hangs a small brass plaque that reads *Sinking ship—here's the last drink*. The bar manager invites us to help ourselves to sandwiches, great doorstops of bread filled with ham and cheese. We play a round of pool as Bruce Springsteen sings "Born to Run" on the jukebox. Fortner is good and wins handily, but his energy is flagging. In addition to AIDS he has epilepsy, and he begins to worry that he might experience a seizure. We head back to his building, taking a route that is familiar to Fortner from his days offering sex for money. A train rumbles above on an elevated stretch of the subway. Fortner points to a 24-hour laundromat. "I used to hang out there a lot," he says.

After his diagnosis, Fortner got so sick that he wound up in a nursing home with four blood clots in each leg, unable to walk for months. "I went from being confined to bed, having my Pampers changed, to a wheelchair to a walker to crutches and then a cane."

One of the ways in which HASA works is that recipients have to have a T-cell count below 200—the level at which AIDS is diagnosed—to be eligible for benefits, encouraging potential recipients to let their health deteriorate to dangerous levels. Fortner sums up his own process of coaxing his HIV into full-blown AIDS as: "Don't take no meds, don't go to a doctor. And that's what I did. I sabotaged myself to get my numbers down."

Fortner also started abusing heroin and crystal meth. "I was doing every drug and my drinking was crazy," he says. He also became more sexually promiscuous: "I kind of slept with anyone and did anything they wanted to do with me."

The plan worked. In 2008 he became eligible for housing, financial aid, free healthcare, and food stamps. Once he reached entitlement he could keep his benefits even if his health improved, so he started taking his pills.

After spending his life in dozens of different houses and shelters, Fortner finally had his own apartment. "It felt like heaven when I walked in," he says. "I'm still in shock that I actually got my apartment. If I didn't have my apartment I would probably still be a sex worker."

Temi Aregbesola was the director of prevention and outreach programs at the Bronx Community Pride Center, an organization that served LGBT youth until it closed in the summer of 2012 due to economic strife. She has often broken the diagnosis of HIV to young gay men, ages 16 and older, and has been shocked by some of the responses. "'Oh, if I have HIV, I'm good, they will take care of me. I'm going to get housing, I'm going to get my meds,'" Aregbesola paraphrases. "Outside their world, there is still a lot of stigma. But in their world, [it's] 'Oh, I got the monster? This is now an opportunity for me to be better than I was last year.'"

For Johnny Guaylupo, a program coordinator for Housing Works, which connects New Yorkers living with HIV to primary care and social services, the best way to help young people avoid the vicious cycle in which Fortner and others have found themselves is to get them off the streets and into subsidized housing sooner, thereby reducing their likelihood of engaging in risky behavior. Even if they already have HIV, housing can help them live longer. "If you have stable housing, you're able to at least take your medication, eat nutritious meals, get enough sleep, and not go through the stress of living in the streets or having to sell your body," he says.

Since March 2011, Guaylupo has been responsible for targeting homeless LGBT youth between the age of 13 and 24 who are infected or are at risk of becoming infected with HIV. The aim is to link them to emergency housing, medical care, HIV testing, counseling, and other supportive services. They also try to map certain trends. "Are they going out clubbing? Are they doing sex work? Are they doing sex work online, and if they are, where?" he says. The rise of the Internet has moved much prostitution off the streets and onto sites such as Rentboy.com, and although there are no statistics of homeless youth sex workers in New York City, Guaylupo believes it could be in the thousands.

Aregbesola worries that not enough is being done to prevent youth from becoming infected with HIV, and warns that the outlook is getting worse. "A lot of HIV prevention funding has been slashed by the New York State Department of Health," she says. At the same time,

HIV infection rates are on the rise. At the end of last year, the CDC issued a report that showed that HIV infection rates from 2008–2010 rose 12% for all gay men—and a staggering 22% for young gay men. More than half of those (55%) were black men. "It really breaks my heart," says Aregbesola. "It is a chronic illness—there is no cure. Unless you have some type of magnificent immune system, you will be on meds for pretty much the bulk of your life."

Rivera, too, believes that HIV could have been prevented in those young men who are grateful for the disease if only there had been the resources to reach them. "It could have been if they had had the proper tools, education about what HIV and AIDS is and how it's spread," he says, adding that many young gay men also feel alienated from social programs designed to help them find jobs and develop vocational skills.

Fortner's story is typical of this narrative. "You live in the moment," he says, "and you feel like, *I'm not going to be shit, so I might as well just get high and numb everything I'm feeling—I'm not going to get rescued, this is going to be my reality for life.* You really feel that way."

Born in Albany, Fortner was taken into foster care at the age of 14. His parents, addicted to crack, were unable to look after him and his eight younger brothers and sisters. By the time he was 17, he was living in Green Chimneys, a temporary housing center in New York City for homeless LGBT youth. At night he would join up with a group of transgender sex workers, dressing in dark blue skinny jeans, a button-up blouse, and high heels. He painted his face with purple eye shadow and shiny lip gloss and embellished the look with false eyelashes. His purse was filled with condoms and weapons such as a hammer, a screwdriver, and a blade.

"You'd get a lot of assholes that wanted to take advantage of me without paying," he says. "A few times a gun was pulled on me, but you threaten to expose them or call the police, and they either give you the money or take off running." One night he had sex with 14 men. "I could do it without alcohol or drugs, but it was a lot easier to do when I was high or drunk," he says.

In 2007, the Empire State Coalition undertook the first comprehensive study of homeless youth between the ages of 13 to 24 in New York City, and found that, on any given night, more than 3,800 youth were homeless on the streets of New York City, with a fairly even

Homeless AIDS patients can get government assistance for food stamps, housing, and health care. Critics say that such assistance has led to an increase in infections.

male-female split. Of them, 44.5% were African American and 28% identified as LGBT, with a further 11% unsure of their orientation or uncomfortable answering the question. The number of homeless youth in New York may be higher now, in the wake of a crippling recession. Covenant House's Nancy Downing, for one, claims she has seen an uptick in requests for shelter.

"We have on any given night about 300 youths staying here," she says. "I know that on a monthly basis we get at least 300 inquiries where we cannot respond and provide them with shelter."

State limits mean that young people can stay in runaway and homeless youth shelters for 30 days, and an additional 30 days with permission from the county youth bureau. After that, they are often on the streets again. "When they can't get a space, they're sleeping in Port Authority—they're finding places to sleep where people can't find them," says Downing. "They're sleeping under bridges, they're sleeping in alleyways, they're sleeping in stairwells."

Even in shelters they can be exposed to danger. "Gang recruitment happens in shelters," Downing says. "Pimps and traffickers also send in young people to recruit. They know that kids are leaving the shelter here, so they'll stand on the corner and try to convince youth that they'll be better off if they engage in prostitution—they'll have more money in their pockets. It's difficult to identify who's doing what, because the young person who is being sent in here may also be a victim of prostitution and trafficking." By addressing the issues and advising the youth, Covenant House tries to make them more aware of the dangers within their surroundings.

The high representation of homeless LGBT youth in New York City is not surprising to Boris Dittrich, LGBT rights advocacy director for Human Rights Watch. "LGBT youth deal with a lot of discrimination, especially in rural areas of the United States. Once the bullying at home leads them to run away, they all move to the bigger cities," he says, adding that New York needs to focus on prevention. "The education system should focus more on sexual diversity. That's not happening enough, and often is stopped by Republicans and religious groups."

James Bolas, of the Empire State Coalition, acknowledges that Mayor Michael Bloomberg has done more for homeless youth in New York City than former mayor Rudy Giuliani did, but says it's not good enough. "Homeless adolescents are then going to become homeless adults and become a burden on the medical system, the mental health system, the detention system, and the correctional system," he says. "They don't understand that if you can catch and serve effectively from the beginning, you prevent it from taxing society on the end."

The equation is simple, Bolas says: Homeless LGBT youth need the things that anyone needs to live. "To have transportation, to not worry about where their next meal is going to come from," he says. "To have the skills to learn a trade, to earn money. To be able to socialize with people safely and not have to be looking over their shoulders." But the most important thing, according to Bolas, is "to have a place where they can sleep and where their door locks."

Fortner can vouch for that. He still has bad days—"Sometimes I don't even get out of bed," he says—but for the first time in a long time he is looking ahead to his future.

Like his idol, Whitney Houston, he sings gospel music in a local church choir and hopes to develop a music career. He is working on getting some headshots, and says he'll dye his hair cinnamon brown to cover some of the marks left by a violent lover who took a crowbar to his head, putting him in a coma for five days. That was back in Albany, shortly before he was diagnosed with HIV and a world away from his life in the Bronx today.

"I kind of created a new family here," he says. "I have a gay father and a gay mother. I met them through a friend of mine and they just took a liking to me. I said, 'You know what? You're going to be my gay mother and you're going to be my gay father.' They've been there for me for years now."

Back at his apartment, he pauses. "I never thought I'd be able to make it here as long as I have," he says. "It's a good feeling." He turns and makes his way slowly up the steps of his building, his home.

EVALUATING THE AUTHOR'S ARGUMENTS:

After reading Maral Noshad Sharifi's viewpoint discussing the connection between government assistance and AIDS infection as well as the previous viewpoint by Peter Staley about infection rates and the gay rights movement, do you see any connections between the two? What do you believe to be the most important issues within the gay community regarding the spread of AIDS, and how do you think these issues should be addressed?

Binge Drinking Increases Women's Risk of Contracting an STD

Rick Nauert

"We found . . . that binge drinking increased STD risk for women."

In the viewpoint that follows Rick Nauert presents the results of a study whose authors argue that women binge drinkers are more likely to engage in risky sexual behaviors that could lead to a sexually transmitted disease (STD) than are men who binge drink and women who do not binge drink. This study, conducted at the Johns Hopkins University School of Medicine, examined the behaviors of nearly eight hundred STD clinic patients and found that the women who binge drank engaged in risky sexual behaviors with greater frequency than did their male counterparts. The authors found that in addition to taking part in these sexual acts, women were also more likely to contract an STD due to differences in male and female anatomy.

Nauert is an associate professor at the Texas State University School of Health Administration who has extensive experience in both clinical and health information positions.

A new study finds a strong link between binge drinking (5+ alcoholic beverages at one time) and risky sexual behaviors. The study is one of the few to examine this association by gender in an urban clinic for sexually transmitted diseases (STDs).

Results show that binge drinking among women attending the clinic was linked to unsafe sexual practices—such as multiple partners and anal sex—and high rates of gonorrhea.

Results [were] published in the November [2008] issue of *Alcoholism: Clinical & Experimental Research.* . . .

Many Are Unaware of the Risks of Binge Drinking

"The link between binge drinking and risky sexual behavior is complex," said Heidi E. Hutton, assistant professor of psychiatry and behavioral sciences at Johns Hopkins University School of Medicine as well as corresponding author for the study.

"We wanted to examine one component of that relationship, whether binge drinking increased the risk of engaging in sexual behaviors and having STDs.

We found gender differences in binge drinking among patients at an STD clinic, and also that binge drinking increased STD risk for women."

"Binge drinking results in a decreased ability to make clear decisions," noted Geetanjali Chander, assistant professor of medicine in the division of general internal medicine at Johns Hopkins University School of Medicine, "and can enable individuals to engage in behaviors that they would not if sober."

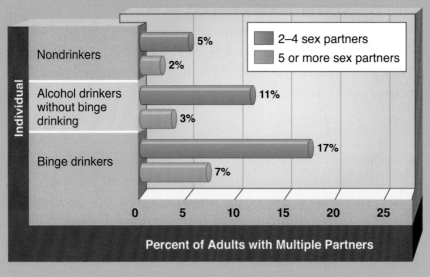

Number of Sex Partners by Alcohol Use for Individuals Living in New York City

- 2–4 sex partners
- 5 or more sex partners

Nondrinkers: 5%, 2%

Alcohol drinkers without binge drinking: 11%, 3%

Binge drinkers: 17%, 7%

Individual

Percent of Adults with Multiple Partners

Taken from: New York City Department of Health and Mental Hygiene. "Health Department Report Links Heavy Drinking to Increased Risk of HIV and Other STDs," January 5, 2009. www.nyc.gov.

Initially, some individuals may drink with the expectation of decreasing inhibitions, or some may drink because they are anxious, or depressed, and they expect alcohol to alleviate their symptoms. Regardless of why they choose to drink, many people do not perceive the potential risk or harm that may result from binge drinking.

Women Suffer More Negative Consequences from Binge Drinking

Between July 2000 and August 2001, researchers approached 795 STD-clinic patients being evaluated/treated for STDs. Of those approached, 671 (322 males, 349 females; 95% African American, 83% heterosexual) agreed to answer questions about their recent alcohol/drug use and risky sexual behaviors using audio computer-assisted self-interview technology.

The association between binge drinking and sexual behaviors/STDs was then analyzed, adjusting for age, employment, and drug use.

"We found that binge drinking among women STD-clinic patients is associated with certain risky sexual behaviors," said Hutton.

"Across gender, women binge drinkers are more likely to have anal sex than men binge drinkers. Within gender, women binge drinkers are three times as likely to have anal sex, and twice as likely to have multiple sex partners compared to women who do not drink alcohol. Compared to non-drinking women, women binge drinkers are also five times as likely to have gonorrhea."

"Gonorrhea is a sexually transmitted disease which reflects unsafe sexual practices," added Chander. "This association between binge drinking and high-risk sexual behaviors is especially important as risky behaviors are associated with HIV acquisition and transmission."

Hutton said that both binge drinking and risky sexual behaviors are more hazardous to women than [to] men.

"If women and men consume the same dose of alcohol, women will have a higher concentration of alcohol in their system, and substantially greater alcohol-caused impairment than men," she said.

"Furthermore, anatomical differences place women at greater risk than men of contracting some sexually transmitted infections. As a result, men transmit some infections to women more efficiently than women do to men.

For example, men are eight to 10 times more likely to transmit HIV to a female partner through repeated, unprotected sexual intercourse than women are to transmit the virus to men."

FAST FACT

A 2012 study by Maria R. Khan at the University of Maryland School of Public Health found that in white adolescents, a history of drinking suggested an individual was 50 percent more likely to have had sex with more than two people in the previous year. As the amount of drinking increased, the likelihood of having more than five sexual partners increased to 70 percent.

"While other studies have demonstrated that alcohol use is associated with high-risk behaviors, this study demonstrates a gender-specific association between binge drinking and risky behaviors which merits further exploration," said Chander.

The author cites a study that found that women who binge drink were at greater risk of contracting an STD.

"Linking binge drinking to an actual biological marker that reflects high-risk sexual behaviors strengthens the argument that alcohol use is associated with high-risk behaviors."

Hutton and her colleagues recommend that clinicians at STD clinics routinely screen for binge drinking.

"While it is standard practice in most STD clinics to discuss behavioral factors for STD risk," said Hutton, "binge drinkers may be harder to identify than alcohol-dependent individuals because the latter have more obvious impairment of function."

EVALUATING THE AUTHOR'S ARGUMENTS:

After reviewing the findings of the Johns Hopkins University study connecting binge drinking to risky sexual behaviors, as reported by viewpoint author Rick Nauert, do you think the study authors proved binge drinking to be the cause of risky sexual behaviors or do you think that people who engage in risky sexual behaviors might also be binge drinkers? Explain your answer.

Senior Citizens' Aging and Lack of Medical Screening May Lead to the Spread of STDs

Elizabeth Boskey

"Numerous factors have contributed to the increase in sexually transmitted diseases in the elderly."

Sexually transmitted diseases (STDs) are no longer just a problem that affects young people, according to Elizabeth Boskey in the viewpoint that follows. Boskey argues that age does not protect people from contracting an STD and, in fact, elderly people may be more likely than their younger counterparts to become infected with an STD. Their increased risk stems from a number of factors identified by the author, including inadequate screening for diseases, lack of awareness about the dangers of STDs, and physiological changes that increase susceptibility to disease. Boskey maintains that these factors combine to create a situation in which STDs are likely to spread and that only through a renewed focus on this population will this problem be overcome.

Elizabeth Boskey, "STDs & the Elderly: Age Is Not a Condom: Old Sex Does Not Mean Safe Sex," About.com, February 8, 2012. Republished with permission.

Boskey is an assistant professor at the State University of New York Downstate Medical Center who teaches, researches, and writes about human sexual behavior with a focus on sexually transmitted diseases.

AS YOU READ, CONSIDER THE FOLLOWING QUESTIONS:
1. What percentage of individuals over sixty have sex at least once a month, according to the author?
2. What do the CDC screening guidelines suggest with regard to who should be screened for HIV and how often, according to Boskey?
3. As stated by the author, why do cervical cancer rates rise in older women?

Sexually transmitted diseases aren't just a problem of the young. Older people can suffer from them, too. In fact, there are several reasons why older adults may actually be in more danger from STDs than their younger companions, including:

1. Lack of screening for sexual problems can increase the risk of a disease going unnoticed for years, leading to serious complications.
2. After menopause, women's vaginal tissues thin and natural lubrication decreases. This can increase the risk of micro-tears and of sexual transmission of certain diseases such as HIV/AIDS.
3. Older people are less likely to use condoms, both because they don't consider themselves to be at risk of STDs and because they were never educated that condoms should be part of their sex lives.
4. The immune system naturally becomes less effective as people age, which can also increase the risk of sexually transmitted infections.

People of All Ages Must Be Taught About Safe-Sex Practices

More than 60% of individuals over 60 have sex at least once a month, and yet they are rarely considered to be "at risk" of an STD. Even those who are no longer sexually active may still have a sexually transmitted infection for which they were never treated or screened, and the long-term neurological side effects of diseases such as HIV and syphilis may be easily mistaken for other diseases of aging.

It is therefore essential that not only older adults, but the individuals who care for them, be educated about STD risk in the elderly. Older individuals, and their caregivers, need to be taught about safer sex, so that they know how to reduce their risk if, and when, they choose to engage in sexual activity. Sex can be an important part of a person's life, no matter what their age. It's important that everyone learn how to engage in it safely so that it enhances their health rather than damaging it.

STD Studies Have Ignored the Elderly

Recent statistics from the CDC [Centers for Disease Control and Prevention] have shown that the number of new HIV infections is actually growing faster in individuals over 50 than in people 40 years and under, and HIV may just be the tip of the iceberg. Numerous factors have contributed to the increase in sexually transmitted diseases in the elderly, and many of them stem from a single problem. Namely, clinicians and scientists don't spend enough time thinking, or talking, about older individuals having sex. Not only are the elderly usually overlooked in many STD studies, but they are frequently less likely to get screened for STDs than their younger counterparts.

> **FAST FACT**
>
> In 2009 data from the Centers for Disease Control and Prevention showed that 32.7 percent of individuals diagnosed and living with HIV were age fifty or older. This is a 14.3 percent increase from 2007.

Part of the problem, at least, is addressed by the new CDC screening guidelines which, among other things, recommend that health care providers screen all patients between the ages of 13 and 64 for HIV as part of their regular visits. In this age, when divorce rates are up and Viagra and other erectile dysfunction medications are available online, sex among the elderly may be at an all-time high.

Older Women Do Not Get Screened for HPV

Every year, thousands of women in the United States die from cervical cancer. Most of these deaths should never occur. Cervical cancer

Sexually active older people may be more at risk for contracting an STD due to a lack of screening among this population, so consultation with a physician is encouraged.

is largely a preventable disease. Caused by the sexually transmitted virus HPV [human papillomavirus], regular cervical screening via Pap smear is an effective way to catch early cancerous changes before they can start to cause problems.

One of the many reasons why the incidence of cervical cancer rises so quickly in older women is that many women, once they stop needing birth control pills, stop going to their gynecologist. Although Pap smears can be done by any clinician, many older women are reluctant to seek out the discomfort of a sexual health exam, particularly if they are unmarried, not sexually active, post-menopausal, under-insured, or have a limited income. Older women may also be reluctant to be screened for something that, in its early stages, has no symptoms and for which they perceive themselves to be at little risk.

Screening, however, is essential. It can take a decade or more for an HPV infection to develop into the early stages of cervical cancer. Although screening guidelines vary by organization, in general, even older women who are not sexually active should still be considered to be at risk. . . .

Most women will need to be tested once a year, but certain women who are considered to be at very low risk may be able to reduce their screening requirements to once every two or three years. If you have a woman in your family, a mother or a grandmother, of that age, make certain she knows she needs to be regularly tested. It could save her life.

EVALUATING THE AUTHOR'S ARGUMENTS:

After reading Elizabeth Boskey's article about the increased rate of STD infection in older adults and learning that new HIV infection rates are growing faster in this population, what do you see as the impact of education on solving this problem? Do you think that more education about STDs when individuals are young will prevent them from engaging in behaviors that could put them at risk as they age? Why or why not?

The Risk of Contracting an STD Increases with Pubic Hair Removal

Joseph M. Mercola

"New research suggests shaving your pubic hair may actually increase your risk of contracting a sexually transmitted disease."

In the viewpoint that follows Joseph M. Mercola argues that pubic hair removal leads to an increased risk of sexually transmitted disease (STD) infection. He points to a new study showing that most individuals in the sample who removed their hair contracted the molluscum virus and experienced other STDs and skin problems. The author notes that this study is not an isolated case and that another physician has noticed the same trend in her own practice. Mercola concludes that the increased risk for STD infection combined with the health functions of pubic hair make removal of one's pubic hair a less attractive option.

Mercola is an osteopathic doctor certified in family medicine who combines both traditional and natural medicine in his practice. He is a published author and runs the popular health website Mercola.com.

AS YOU READ, CONSIDER THE FOLLOWING QUESTIONS:
1. What are some of the "other skin issues" noted by the researchers in the pubic hair removal study cited by the author?
2. How does the molluscum virus spread, according to Mercola?
3. What four functions does Mercola state that hair on the body serves?

According to a recent survey, a large percentage of US college students remove some or all of their pubic hair,[1] as does a sizable portion of the rest of the population. It's a growing trend that may actually have ancient roots, as pubic hair removal was thought to have been practiced among women in ancient Greece, Egypt and Rome.[2]

In modern times, both men and women use a variety of methods (shaving, waxing, clipping, lasers) to remove pubic hair, and describe various motivations for doing so.

Among women, the most popular reasons include the belief that it looks better in a bathing suit, increases feelings of attractiveness, feels more comfortable and the belief that it's cleaner.

Ironically, this latter reasoning may be contradictory, as new research suggests shaving your pubic hair may actually increase your risk of contracting a sexually transmitted disease (STD) known as molluscum contagiosum.

The Viral STD Risk of Shaving Your Pubic Hair

Shaving or waxing can cause irritation and micro-trauma to your skin that increases your risk of contracting a viral infection. Researchers of a new case study observed that the number of cases of molluscum contagiosum have risen along with rates of pubic hair removal.

To look into the link, they observed 30 patients at a private skin care clinic in Nice, France, all of whom were infected with the molluscum virus. Nearly all of them had removed their pubic hair, the vast majority by shaving, followed by waxing and then clipping.

The finding supports the researchers theory that hairless genitals may provide an opportunity for sexually transmitted diseases like molluscum to take hold, with shaving showing the strongest association.

Molluscum contagiosum is spread easily, and the researchers suggested the virus may have spread primarily through self-infection caused by scratching skin irritated by shaving. Other skin issues were also noted among the study participants, which may also have been related to the pubic hair removal. These included:

- Warts (the researchers suggested shaving your pubic hair may also increase the risk of genital warts caused by the human papillomavirus (HPV))
- Bacterial skin infections
- Scars
- Ingrown hairs

People who remove their pubic hair have a greater chance of contracting molluscum virus, a type of pox virus that shows up on the infected area as red lesions.

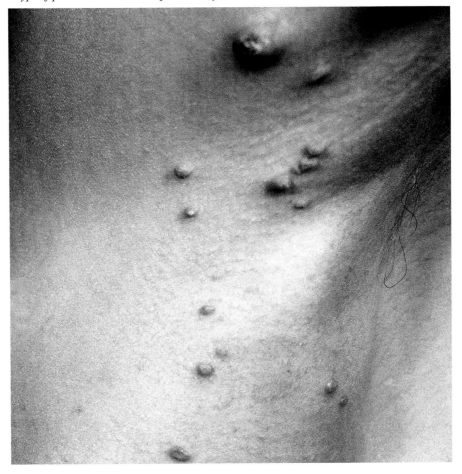

What is Molluscum Contagiosum?

Despite its prevalence, molluscum contagiosum is one of the lesser-known STDs. A type of pox virus, molluscum is actually most common in children, although it also affects adults with weakened immune systems and can be spread through sexual contact. The virus causes firm, pearl-like bumps on the skin, which, though painless, can become easily red and inflamed.

If the bumps are scratched, the infection spreads easily person-to-person as well as through contaminated objects. Shaving over the bumps can also cause the virus to spread. In most cases the infection will resolve within six to 12 months with no treatment, so keeping your immune system strong is important. The bumps can also be removed to help prevent spread of the infection.

Other STDs and Infections May Also Be Linked to Pubic Hair Removal

Is the spread of viruses like molluscum contagiosum and the human papillomavirus the only downside to removing your pubic hair, or are there other consequences? Quite possibly, yes. Last year, a family physician called for an end to the "war on pubic hair," claiming the practice of removing pubic hair increases risks of infection and sexually transmitted diseases. As reported by *The Independent:*[3]

As director of the health centre at Western University in Washington State, US, she has seen the consequences. "Pubic hair removal naturally irritates and inflames the hair follicles, leaving microscopic open wounds. Frequent hair removal is necessary to stay smooth, causing regular irritation of the shaved or waxed area. When that

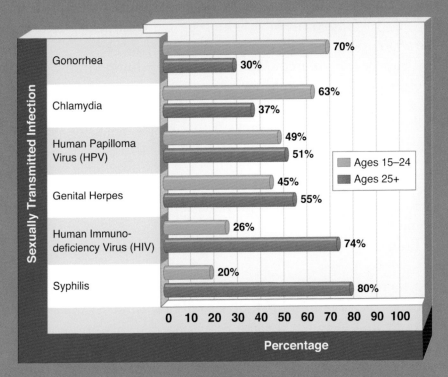

Taken from: Centers for Disease Controland Prevention. *Sexually Transmitted Infections Among Young Americans*, 2013.

is combined with the warm, moist environment of the genitals, it becomes a happy culture media for some of the nastiest bacterial pathogens." . . .

In her practice it is not unusual to find patients with boils and abscesses on their genitals from shaving as well as cellulitis, an infection of the scrotum, labia or penis from shaving or from having sex with someone infected. Herpes is also an increased risk "due to the microscopic wounds being exposed to virus carried by mouth or genitals." "It follows that there may be vulnerability to the spread of other sexually transmitted diseases as well," she says.

Does Pubic Hair Have a Purpose?

The hairless ideal sought by so many people is in truth both unattainable and probably not entirely healthful. Body hair will always grow back (even laser hair removal will only subdue hair growth and thickness by 50 percent or so with repeated treatments), and each time you remove the hair you're causing some damage to your skin. Plus, hair does serve important functions, including in the genital region, such as:

- Protection: helping to prevent foreign particles like dust and pathogenic bacteria from entering your body
- Temperature control: hair captures the air surrounding your body to reduce the loss of heat
- Reduces friction, which prevents skin irritation, abrasion and injury
- Promotes touch reception

So there are some arguments for keeping your pubic hair, and it's likely that a reduced risk of sexually transmitted infections is one of them. Of course, the best way to prevent the spread of STDs is to follow safe-sex practices, or wait to have sex until you're in a committed relationship. Then, keep your immune system in tip-top shape, and it will be better able to fight off any viruses that do come its way. That said, if you're in a committed relationship in which the threat of STDs has been removed, then there is probably little harm in shaving your pubic hair, if that is your preference. (And there is one potential benefit that we haven't discussed: a much lower risk of pubic lice.)

Sources and References

- Sexually Transmitted Infections March 19, 2013
- Medical News Today March 19, 2013
- WebMD March 18, 2013
- [1] October 2011, Volume 65, Issue 7–8, pp 506–517
- [2] The Sex Information and Education Council of Canada, Female Pubic Hair Removal
- [3] The Independent August 5, 2012

EVALUATING THE AUTHOR'S ARGUMENTS:

Joseph M. Mercola presents the results of a study of thirty patients at a private skin care clinic in France to support his claim that pubic hair removal can increase the incidence of STDs. Do you believe that thirty is a large enough sample size to draw conclusions about the connection between STD infection and pubic hair removal? Does the additional experience of the family physician cited by the author provide sufficient additional support to his argument, or is more information needed to draw a valid conclusion? Explain.

Chapter 2

What Education Programs Address the Spread of STDs?

STD information appears on a university bulletin board. Education is the key to lessening one's chances of catching an STD, many argue.

Comprehensive Sex Education Helps to Prevent the Spread of STDs

"Comprehensive [sex education] programs have reduced the self-reported incidence and frequency of unprotected sex and the number of sex partners."

Harvey V. Fineberg

In the following viewpoint the president of the Institute of Medicine, Harvey V. Fineberg, argues that comprehensive sex education programs have been shown in study reviews to be effective at reducing risky sexual behaviors in adolescents that could lead to sexually transmitted infections. Fineberg also asserts that these same reviews have revealed that abstinence-only sex education programs exhibit limited to no effectiveness in influencing teens to refrain from sex. On the basis of these findings, the author contends that additional studies should be conducted to confirm these results and that policies to deter adolescent sex and prevent STDs be created using the evidence from existing and future studies.

Harvey V. Fineberg, "Domestic Abstinence-Only Pograms: Assessing the Evidence," Statement Before the Committee on Oversight and Government Reform, US House of Representatives, April 23, 2008.

AS YOU READ, CONSIDER THE FOLLOWING QUESTIONS:
1. According to the author, how much money was spent on abstinence-only education in 2007 as compared with the total spent in 1997?
2. What are the adverse effects of one abstinence-only program cited by the author?
3. How many comprehensive sex education programs were found to have had an effect on behavioral outcomes reported by participants, according to the review cited by Fineberg?

S ex education programs for adolescents in the U.S. vary considerably in their goals, content, duration and intensity, implementation setting, target age and population, the training and skill of the program facilitator, and other factors. Recognizing these variations, it will be convenient for our purposes to consider sex education curricula in two broad categories: abstinence-only programs and comprehensive programs. Abstinence-only programs (also referred to as "abstinence-until-marriage" programs) teach and encourage young people to remain abstinent from sexual activity as the exclusive method to reduce their risks of HIV, other sexually transmitted infections [STIs], and unintended pregnancy. These programs provide little or no information about safer sex practices or contraception or emphasize their failure rates. Most comprehensive programs for youth (also sometimes referred to as "abstinence plus" programs) promote abstinence as the best means of preventing HIV, but also educate youth about correct and consistent use of condoms and other contraception to reduce unintended pregnancy, and to decrease the risk of contracting HIV or other infections.

Funding for abstinence-only programs has increased significantly in the past decade since the enactment of the Personal Responsibility and Work Opportunity Reconciliation Act ("welfare reform act") in 1996. This legislation created a new State Abstinence Education Program, funded through section 510 of the Social Security Act for abstinence-only education, appropriating $50 million per year for five years. The program has been reauthorized under extensions of the welfare reform act. Other significant sources of federal funding for abstinence-only education include the Community Based Abstinence Education

(CBAE) program and the Adolescent and Family Life (AFL) Program. Together, these three programs (Title V, CBAE, and AFL) totaled $176 million in federal funding for abstinence-only education in FY [fiscal year] 2007 (state funding excluded)—compared to the $9 million in federal funding in FY 1997 prior to the enactment of the welfare reform act. Obtaining comparable estimates of expenditures on comprehensive sex education programs is difficult because funding for these programs comes from multiple state, local, federal and private funding streams that are mixed with funding for other services. In light of what are surely substantial expenditures for both types of programs, it is reasonable to ask how well they achieve their goals.

Self-Reported Behavioral Measures Determine a Program's Success

In the 2001 IOM [Institute of Medicine] report *No Time to Lose: Getting More from HIV Prevention,* an expert committee reviewed the scientific evidence on the effectiveness of abstinence-only and comprehensive sex education programs targeting youth in preventing HIV

This public service poster in Los Angeles is part of an STD awareness program and urges people to get tested.

infection. At the time, the committee concluded that evidence was insufficient to determine whether abstinence programs were effective in reducing sexual activity, in part because many programs had yet to be rigorously evaluated. In contrast, multiple reviews concluded that comprehensive sex education programs were effective in reducing self-reported high-risk sexual behaviors among adolescents and that they did not increase self-reported sexual activity.

Today we have an opportunity to assess what the cumulative evidence in 2008 tells us about the effectiveness of these programs in preventing HIV transmission. . . .

The majority of studies on the effectiveness of abstinence-only and comprehensive programs examine self-reported measures of behavior rather than attempting to measure reductions in the incidence of disease or pregnancy. Self-reported behavioral outcome measures are not as strong as objective biological measures because they are an imperfect reflection of actual behavior and subject to bias.

Relevant behavioral outcome measures for programs to prevent HIV include: abstinence (or return to abstinence) from sex; reductions in the frequency of unprotected vaginal, anal, and oral sex or increases in condom use; reductions in the number of sexual partners and avoidance of concurrent partners; regular screening and treatment for STIs; and vaccination for certain STIs (HPV [human papillomavirus] and hepatitis B).

Abstinence-Only Sex Education Programs Show Little Effect on Behavior

In the Cochrane review [by the medical information systematizing organization the Cochrane Collaboration] of abstinence-only programs, no program showed an effect on incidence of unprotected vaginal sex, number of sex partners, condom use or sexual initiation compared to controls. One trial favored an abstinence-only program over usual care for incidence of vaginal sex, but this was limited to two-month follow-up and was offset by measurement error and six other studies with non-significant effects. One evaluation found several significant adverse program effects: abstinence-only participants in this program were more likely than usual-care controls to report sexually transmitted infections, pregnancy and increased frequency of vaginal sex. Overall, the authors concluded that abstinence-only programs neither reduced nor exacerbated HIV risk among participants in the U.S.

One of the most rigorous recent evaluations of federally funded abstinence-only programs was completed in 2007 by Mathematics Policy Research, Inc. This was a multi-year, experimentally-based impact evaluation of four federally-funded abstinence-only sex education programs funded under from Title V, Section 510 of Personal Responsibility and Work Opportunity Reconciliation Act of 1996. These four programs vary in their strategies, settings, and population characteristics. Participants in these programs were randomized to abstinence-only program or control conditions. Based on follow-up data collected 4–6 years after enrollment, youth in the abstinence-only program group were no more likely to have abstained from sex compared to those enrolled in the control group. Among those who reported having had sex, the group receiving abstinence-only education reported having similar numbers of sexual partners and similar timing of onset of sexual debut to those in the control group. The abstinence-only program participants were no more likely to have engaged in unprotected sex than youth in the control group.

> **FAST FACT**
>
> Research cited by the Sexuality Information and Education Council of the United States reports that students who participate in comprehensive sex education programs wait longer to have sexual intercourse, are more likely to use condoms or other forms of contraception during sex, and have fewer sexual partners.

Comprehensive Sex Education Programs Are Effective at Changing Behavior

In the Cochrane review of comprehensive sex education programs for youth in high-income countries, 23 of the 39 trials found a positive effect on at least one self-reported behavioral outcome including sexual abstinence, condom use, and unprotected sex. While the specific features that contribute most to success are difficult to discern because of the variable design in these programs, the review found

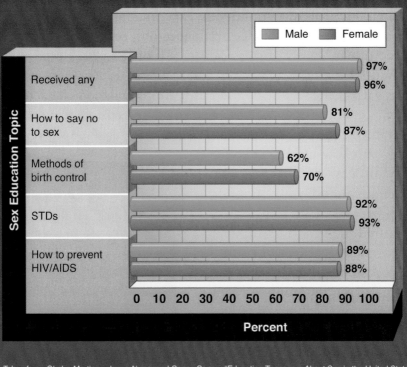

Percent of American Teens Who Received Sex Education When They Were Fifteen to Nineteen, by Topic and Sex, from 2006–2008

Male   Female

Received any
97%
96%

How to say no to sex
81%
87%

Methods of birth control
62%
70%

STDs
92%
93%

How to prevent HIV/AIDS
89%
88%

0   10   20   30   40   50   60   70   80   90   100

Sex Education Topic

Percent

Taken from: Gladys Martinez, Joyce Abma, and Casey Copen. "Educating Teenagers About Sex in the United States." NCHS Data Brief, no. 44, September 2010.

many comprehensive sex education programs appear to reduce self-reported short-term and long-term HIV-risk behaviors among young people in high income countries. These findings of positive behavioral outcomes are consistent with a prior independent review of the same body of literature.

In the seven years since *No Time to Lose* was published, there is little additional evidence about the impact of sex-education programs that rely on biologically verified reductions in the incidence of HIV and other STIs. The growing body of literature on the impact of sex education programs on behavioral outcomes, however, provides more information.

Based on the relatively small number of rigorous evaluations, abstinence-only programs do not reduce the risk of HIV as measured by self-reported behavioral outcomes. Studies indicate that abstinence-only programs do not result in a delay in the initiation of sexual activity, a reduction in the frequency of unprotected vaginal sex, or a reduction in the number of sexual partners. Among sexually active teens, abstinence-only programs have not been shown to increase the return to sexual abstinence nor to affect condom use.

Comprehensive sex-education programs appear more promising. Several studies found a positive effect on a number of behavioral outcomes. Comprehensive programs have reduced the self-reported incidence and frequency of unprotected sex and the number of sex partners. These programs have also been demonstrated to increase reported condom use and to delay initiation of sexual activity.

Evidence-Based Sex Ed Programs Must Be Implemented

The available evidence on the impact of sex education programs is limited to a relatively small number of well-executed, controlled studies. Future evaluations should endeavor to improve study quality in such areas as program specification, outcome measures, length of follow-up, and retention of study participants. Studies that validated behavioral measures against biological outcomes would be a valuable addition. Especially useful would be studies that compared abstinence-only and comprehensive programs head-to-head in the same target population at the same time.

I believe public funds should support programs that are well grounded in evidence. By this standard, public financing and wide deployment of abstinence-only programs does not constitute sound fiscal or public health policy. Comprehensive sex education programs appear to be more effective, although this conclusion is based mainly on self-reported behavior change rather than on direct biological measures of outcome. Encouraging innovation and flexibility in the design of future sex education programs coupled to a systematic evaluation strategy is the most promising path to reducing HIV and other sexually transmitted infections among adolescents.

Abstinence-Only Sex Education Helps to Prevent the Spread of STDs

"Abstinence is the surest way to avoid the risk of STDs."

Christine Kim and Robert Rector

Christine Kim and Robert Rector, in the following viewpoint, call on the government to reconsider instituting abstinence-only sex education programs in schools to prevent the spread of sexually transmitted diseases (STDs) and unwed pregnancy. The authors argue that abstinence is the most certain way of preventing STDs and teen pregnancy, and numerous studies have shown that abstinence-only education, when implemented strictly according to lesson plans, has been linked to decreased rates of sexual activity in adolescents. They provide overviews of several studies exhibiting these results and detail the samples and findings. While the authors acknowledge that some studies have shown little or no impact, they contend that these studies differ somewhat in their design from the majority of studies on abstinence-only education, and the results showing the programs' benefits cannot be overlooked.

Kim is a policy analyst and Rector a senior research fellow at the conservative public policy organization the Heritage Foundation in Washington, DC.

AS YOU READ, CONSIDER THE FOLLOWING QUESTIONS:
1. According to the authors, what do abstinence-only education programs teach?
2. What did the authors of the study evaluating the abstinence program Reasons of the Heart find with regard to its impact on teen sexual activity, as reported by Kim and Rector?
3. As stated by the authors, how did the Mathematica Policy Research study differ from the field's conventions on time between program completion and follow up?

Teen sexual activity remains a widespread problem confronting the nation. Each year, some 2.6 million teenagers become sexually active—a rate of 7,000 teens per day. Among high school students, nearly half report having engaged in sexual activity, and one-third are currently active.

Sexual activity during teenage years poses serious health risks for youths and has long-term implications. Early sexual activity is associated with an increased risk of sexually transmitted diseases (STDs), reduced psychological and emotional well-being, lower academic achievement, teen pregnancy, and out-of-wedlock childbearing. Many of these risks are avoidable if teens choose to abstain from sexual activity. Abstinence is the surest way to avoid the risk of STDs and unwed childbearing.

Abstinence education "teaches abstinence from sexual activity outside marriage as the expected standard for all school age children" [according to a Department of Health and Human Services fact sheet] and stresses the social, psychological, and health benefits of abstinence. Abstinence programs also provide youths with valuable life and decision-making skills that lay the foundation for personal responsibility and developing healthy relationships and marriages later in life. These programs empha-size preparing young people for future-oriented goals.

Studies have shown that abstinent teens report, on average, bet-ter psychological well-being and higher educational attainment than those who are sexually active. Delaying the initiation of or reducing early sexual activity among teens can decrease their overall exposure to risks of unwed childbearing, STDs, and psycho-emotional harm. Authentic abstinence programs are therefore crucial to efforts aimed at reducing unwed childbearing and improving youth well-being. . . .

Abstinence-Only Programs Vary Greatly

The research field of abstinence program evaluation is developing, so only a handful of programs has been evaluated thus far. Currently, sev-eral hundred abstinence programs are in operation nationwide. These programs vary substantially in the youth populations that they serve, in their implementation, and in their curricula. Importantly, the few evaluated programs inadequately represent the spectrum of abstinence programs. Consequently, the available findings are mostly generaliz-able to the specific conditions under which those particular programs were implemented and to the youth populations that they served. . . .

Experimental studies have the most rigorous evaluation design. A true experiment enables the researchers to draw conclusions about the program's impact with a high degree of confidence. To simulate the scenario of how abstinence program participants would have behaved if they had not received any abstinence education, an experiment ran-domly assigns youths to receive or not to receive abstinence education. In theory, random assignment eliminates any systematic differences between the intervention group and the control group, making the two virtually identical except for the intervention—in this case, abstinence education. In reality, well-designed and well-implemented experiments are few. This is particularly true for abstinence program evaluation.

Most of the evaluations reported in this analysis are quasi-experiments, which incorporate certain elements of experimental design, such as iden-tifying a comparable group of youths for comparison and using statistical methods to account for pre-intervention differences between youths who received abstinence education and those who did not.

Quasi-experimental studies adjust for a host of observable factors other than abstinence education that might confound the results.

Depending on the rigor of the evaluation design and the adequacy of the statistical analysis employed by the researchers, the degree of confidence with which conclusions may be drawn about the findings from non-experimental studies can vary. Consequently, all findings should be interpreted with the full context of the program and evaluation in view. . . .

While abstinence programs emphasize the message of abstinence until marriage as the standard for all school-age children, simply delaying the initiation or reducing current levels of sexual activity among teens can decrease teens' overall exposure to the risk of physical and psycho-emotional harm. . . .

Abstinence-Only Programs Prove More Effective than Other Programs

A 2010 study in the medical journal *Archives of Pediatrics and Adolescent Medicine*, published by the American Medical Association, concludes that an "abstinence-only intervention reduced sexual initiation" as well as recent sexual activity among a group of African-American adolescents. Two years after attending an eight-hour abstinence program, about one-third of the participants had initiated sexual activity, compared to nearly one-half of the non-participants who enrolled in a general health program. That is, the abstinence program reduced the rate of sexual initiation by one-third. Moreover, abstinence program participants who became sexually active were not less likely to use contraception.

By contrast, the study also evaluated two alternative interventions, one that only taught contraception (i.e., the "safe sex" approach) and another that contained both abstinence and contraception content (i.e., comprehensive sex education), and found that neither program delayed or reduced teen sexual activity. Furthermore, these programs, whose main emphasis is on contraception, failed to increase use among adolescents.

The study implemented a randomized controlled experiment, the gold standard for such evaluations. Six hundred sixty-two sixth- and seventh-grade African-American students participated in the experiment. These students attended four public middle schools that served low-income communities in a northeastern U.S. city. Students were randomly assigned to attend an eight-hour abstinence-only program, an eight-hour "safe sex" program that promoted contraception, an eight- or twelve-hour comprehensive sex education program that taught both abstinence and contraception, or an eight-hour general health class without any sex education content, which served as the control group.

Abstinence Alone Is More Effective than Combining Methods

Taught over 20 class periods by certified and program-trained health educators, the Reasons of the Heart (ROH) curriculum focuses on individual character development and teaches adolescents the benefits that are associated with abstinence until marriage.

A 2008 study evaluated the ROH curriculum's impact on adolescent sexual activity among seventh grade students in three suburban northern Virginia public schools. The researchers also collected data on a comparison group of seventh grade students in two nearby middle schools that did not participate in the program. Students in

The authors argue that abstinence-only education has been linked to decreased rates of sexual activity in adolescents and thus helps reduce the spread of STDs.

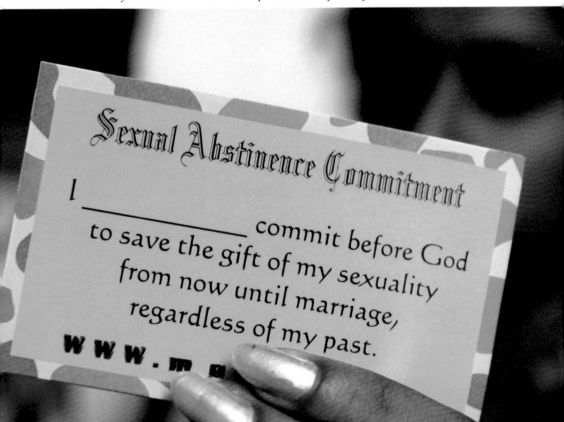

those schools instead received the state's standard family life education, which included two videos on HIV/STD prevention and one on abstinence.

The evaluators surveyed seventh-grade students in all five schools before and after the program. They found that, a year after the program, 32 (9.2 percent) of the 347 ROH students who were virgins at the initial survey had initiated sexual activity, compared with 31 (or 16.4 percent) of the 189 comparison group students. Controlling for the differences between the comparison group and ROH students, the study reported that ROH students were half as likely as comparison group students to initiate sexual activity. The evaluators concluded, "This result appears to compare favorably to the reductions in initiation achieved by some of the abstinence programs [evaluated in earlier studies]."

Abstinence-Only Education Teaches Life Skills

Sex Can Wait is a three-series abstinence education program with one series for upper-elementary students, a second for middle school students, and a third for high school students. The Sex Can Wait program lasts five weeks and offers lessons on character building, important life skills, and reproductive biology.

A 2006 study evaluated the program's long-term (18-month) impact on adolescent sexual behavior. The researchers compared students who participated in Sex Can Wait to those who received their school districts' standard sex education curricula on two behavioral outcomes: overall abstinence and abstinence during the last 30 days. As the authors noted, "the study compared the effects of the Sex Can Wait curriculum to 'current practice' rather than true 'control conditions.'"

The researchers found that, 18 months after the program, upper-elementary students who participated in Sex Can Wait were less likely than non-participants to report engaging in recent sexual activity. Among middle school students, participants were also less likely than non-participants to report engaging in sexual activity ever and in the preceding month before the 18-month follow-up. Finally, among high school students, the authors found reduced levels of sexual activity in the short term but not in the 18-month follow-up.

Middle and High School Students Respond to Abstinence Education

Heritage Keepers is a primary prevention abstinence program for middle school and high school students. The program offers an interactive three-year, two-level curriculum.

To assess Heritage Keepers' impact, a group of evaluators compared some 1,200 virgin students who attended schools that faithfully implemented the program to some 250 students in demographically and geographically comparable schools who did not receive the abstinence intervention. One year after the program, 14.5 percent of Heritage Keepers students had become sexually active compared with 26.5 percent of the comparison group.

Overall, Heritage Keepers students "were about one-half as likely" as comparison group students to initiate sex after adjusting for pre-program differences between the two groups. The study found similar results in subsets of African-American students, Caucasian students, boys, and girls.

Students Are Taught the Negative Impacts of Pregnancy and STDs

A study published in 2005 evaluated the For Keeps curriculum as implemented in five urban and two suburban middle schools in the Midwest. Schools were assigned by the school districts to receive the program, which was part of a county-wide teen pregnancy prevention initiative.

Taught by outside facilitators, For Keeps was a five-day curriculum with 40-minute sessions that focused on character development and

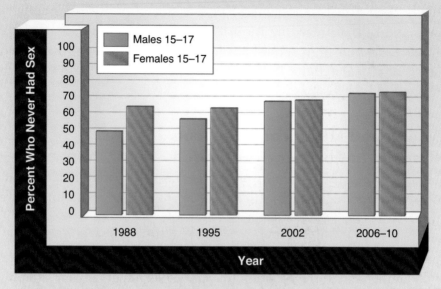

Abstinent Behavior Increases Among Teens Aged Fifteen to Seventeen

Percent Who Never Had Sex

Males 15–17
Females 15–17

100
90
80
70
60
50
40
30
20
10
0

1988   1995   2002   2006–10

Year

Taken from: National Abstinence Education Association. *Abstinence Works 2013: Sexual Risk Avoidance (SRA) Education Programs Demonstrating Improved Teen Outcomes.* Washington, DC: NAEF, 2013.

the benefits of abstinence and tried to help students understand how pregnancy and sexually transmitted diseases can impede their long-term goals. It also emphasized the psycho-emotional and economic consequences of early sexual activity. The curriculum was intended both for students who had become sexually active and for those who had not.

The evaluation collected data on all students through a pretest survey, and some 2,000 youths (about 70 percent of those who took the pretest survey) responded to a follow-up survey conducted about five months after the program ended. Among youths who engaged in any sexual behavior during the follow-up period, some who participated in For Keeps reported a reduction in "the amount of casual sex, as evidenced by fewer episodes of sex and fewer sexual partners" during the evaluation period, although program participants did not differ from non-participants in the likelihood of engaging in sexual activity during the follow-up interval. . . .

One Study Showing No Effect from the Field's Conventions

In 2007, Mathematica Policy Research released a study that evaluated four abstinence programs: My Choice, My Future! in Powhatan, Virginia; ReCapturing the Vision in Miami, Florida; Families United to Prevent Teen Pregnancy in Milwaukee, Wisconsin; and Teens in Control in Clarksdale, Mississippi. Primarily preventive in their intent, these programs focused on upper elementary and middle school children. The average age of the participants ranged from 10 to 13. Two of the sites were in urban settings, and two were in rural communities.

The four programs varied in duration and intensity. Three programs—two multi-year curricula and a one-year curriculum—required participation. Their intensity ranged from several sessions a year to daily classes. One program, an up-to-four-year curriculum, met daily but made participation optional. In that program, only about half of the students assigned to the program actually participated. Of those who participated at all, less than half attended a meaningful portion of the sessions offered.

The evaluation employed a rigorous experimental design. The researchers surveyed students four to six years after initial program enrollment to assess the impact of the four programs on youth behavior. Although long-term impact is ideal, some students in this study's sample were last surveyed later than is conventional in this field. For example, at the program site with the shortest curriculum length (about one year), students averaged about 10 years old at enrollment, and the gap between program completion and the last follow-up survey was as long as five years. During this gap, the students received no additional abstinence education or intervention support.

In the final follow-up survey, the study reported no statistically significant differences between program participants and non-participants. Among both program and control groups, half of the students remained abstinent. Among students who had become sexually active by the time of the final survey, program participants and non-participants had similar rates of condom use. (The four abstinence programs did not promote contraceptive use.)

At one of the program sites, the study found that 48 percent of the program participants remained abstinent in the final follow-up compared with 43 percent of the non-participants. At the same site, program participants were also more likely (a difference of 7 percentage points) to report expectations of abstinence until marriage compared with non-participants. Although these differences were not statistically significant, the study's authors noted that, "[g]iven the smaller sample sizes available for estimate impact at the site level . . . the study cannot rule out modest site-specific impacts on these outcomes." . . .

Abstinence Education Promotes Physical and Psychological Health

Today's young people face strong peer pressure to engage in risky behavior and must navigate media and popular culture that endorse and even glamorize permissiveness and casual sex. Alarmingly, the government implicitly supports these messages by funding programs that promote contraception and "safe-sex."

In FY [fiscal year] 2008, the U.S. Department of Health and Human Services spent $610.1 million on such programs targeting teens—at least four times what it spent on abstinence education. Regrettably, last year [2009], the [Barack] Obama Administration and Congress disregarded the social scientific evidence on abstinence education and eliminated all federal funding for it. Instead, they created additional funding for comprehensive sex education. In his FY2011 budget, the President proposed to increase spending on these programs.

Although 80 percent of parents want schools to teach youths to abstain from sexual activity until they are in a committed adult romantic relationship nearing marriage—the core message of abstinence education—these parental values are rarely communicated in the classroom.

In the classroom, the prevailing mentality often condones teen sexual activity as long as youths use contraceptives. Abstinence is usually mentioned only in passing, if at all. Sadly, many teens who need to learn about the benefits of abstaining from sexual activity during the teenage years never hear them, and many students who choose to abstain fail to receive adequate support for their decisions.

Teen sexual activity is costly, not just for teens, but also for society. Teens who engage in sexual activity risk a host of negative outcomes including STD infection, emotional and psychological harm, lower educational attainment, and out-of-wedlock childbearing.

Genuine abstinence education is therefore crucial to the physical and psycho-emotional well-being of the nation's youth. In addition to teaching the benefits of abstaining from sexual activity until marriage, abstinence programs focus on developing character traits that prepare youths for future-oriented goals.

When considering effective prevention programs aimed at changing teen sexual behavior, lawmakers should consider *all* of the available empirical evidence and restore funding for abstinence education.

EVALUATING THE AUTHORS' ARGUMENTS:

After reading Christine Kim and Robert Rector's article touting the successes of abstinence-only education programs in reducing teen sexual engagement, compare these results with those presented in the viewpoint by Harvey V. Fineberg. Which results do you find more compelling and why? Does one study or set of studies convince you of one program's effectiveness over the other? Why or why not?

Schools Ignore the Value of Abstinence and Restraint by Giving Condoms to Students

Christopher Paslay

"*[Schools] are pushing condoms while refusing to promote values such as abstinence and restraint.*"

In this viewpoint author Christopher Paslay, an educator in the Philadelphia Public School District, argues that students should be taught about abstinence and restraint as well as making condoms available to them. He says that it is important to teach students about restraint because it is a valuable trait for them to possess in resisting sexual impulses as well as other urges young adults may encounter. He maintains that abstinence and restraint are not taught in public schools today because these values have become politicized and associated with conservatism. Paslay teaches at Swenson Arts and Technology High School in Northeast Philadelphia and is the host of the blog

Chalk and Talk. His commentaries on education have appeared in the *Philadelphia Inquirer*, the *Philadelphia Daily News*, and the *City Paper*, among others.

AS YOU READ, CONSIDER THE FOLLOWING QUESTIONS:
  1. According to the author, why is the discussion about abstinence not happening in Philadelphia public schools?
  2. According to the Heritage Keepers Abstinence Education program cited by Paslay, what is the program's main objective?
  3. What does the Buddhist philosopher Thanissaro Bhikku, as cited by Paslay, believe will happen if people do not have restraint?

There are two basic ways to avoid the spread of STDs [sexually transmitted diseases] among high school students: teach them how to practice restraint or give them condoms. The Philadelphia School District and Mayor [Michael] Nutter have chosen to double-down on the latter. In 22 high schools across the city, condoms are now available in clear dispensers outside the nurse's office.

"The reality is, many of our teenagers, regardless of what adults think, are engaged in sexual activities," Mayor Nutter said last week [end of December 2012]. "Discussion about whether or not they should be sexually active is an appropriate discussion, but if they are, then we need to make sure they're engaged in safe sexual practices."

The tragic part of this whole issue is that the discussion about abstaining from sex (practicing restraint) is not happening in Philadelphia public high schools. In fact, the concept of abstinence has been branded as "religious" by those looking to inject politics into the issue of STDs. A closer look at the idea of abstinence (or restraint) reveals it is a value or lifestyle philosophy, not a religious principle. And *values*, such as approaching sex with dignity and reserving it for the most deserving of partners *is* something that should be taught in public schools. Sexual promiscuity comes with consequences, such as HIV and out-of-wedlock births, both of which have a negative impact on education and quality of life.

Kids in public schools should be taught as much. Distributing condoms is fine, but a lesson on restraint should be part of the package;

perhaps there could even be a short *Use Only with That Special Person* on the condom wrapper. But again, those looking to inject politics into the issue rail against any notion of abstinence or restraint. Why? Because abstinence and restraint are viewed as *conservative* and are frequently associated with those who support traditional, heterosexual marriage.

Heritage Keepers Is a Holistic Abstinence Education Program

Earlier this year [2012] President [Barack] Obama, who drastically cut funding for abstinence-only sex education programs in his first term, had a minor change of heart and decided to place Heritage Keepers Abstinence Education Program on the Office of Adolescent Health list of approved groups eligible for government funds. Department of Health and Human Services spokesman Mark Weber said Heritage Keepers had met the criteria, "gone through a transparent, rigorous review process" and had "demonstrated outcomes."

Progressive liberals heard the news and went berserk. According to an article on *Salon*:

> Over a dozen major organizations, including the ACLU [American Civil Liberties Union] and Human Rights Campaign, asked Secretary of Health and Human Services Kathleen Sebelius to explain Heritage Keepers' inclusion. They said the program "ostracizes lesbian, gay, bisexual, and transgender (LGBT) youth; promotes heterosexual marriage as the only acceptable family structure; withholds life-saving information from sexually active youth; and uses fear-based messages to shame youth who have been sexually active and youth living in 'nontraditional' households."

A visit to Heritage Keepers website paints a more inclusive, holistic, and research-based picture of their sex education program, however:

The Heritage Keepers Abstinence Education program encourages teens to develop a strong sense of personal identity and worth, set protective boundaries, resist negative peer pressure, determine and protect personal values and goals, and set high standards for themselves. A significant amount of the curriculum focuses on reproduc-

Abstinent Teens Are More Likely to Finish High School

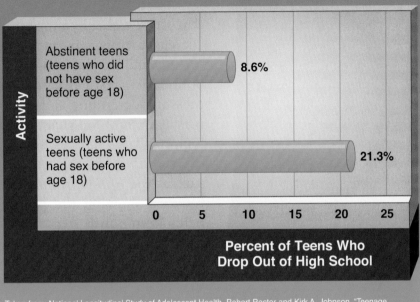

High School Dropout Rates and Teen Sex Activity

Abstinent teens (teens who did not have sex before age 18) — 8.6%

Sexually active teens (teens who had sex before age 18) — 21.3%

Activity

Percent of Teens Who Drop Out of High School

Taken from: National Longitudinal Study of Adolescent Health. Robert Rector and Kirk A. Johnson. "Teenage Sexual Abstinence and Academic Achievement." Heritage Foundation, October 27, 2005. www.heritage.org.

tion and sexually transmitted diseases (STDs), specifically discussing STD symptoms, treatments/cures, and prevention (all with information provided by the Office of Adolescent Pregnancy Prevention and approved for medical accuracy). Condom efficacy is also explained in relation to each STD.

The most recent publication of the Heritage Keepers curriculum in 2008 was approved by the US Department of Health and Human Services, Office of Population Affairs, for medical accuracy and sound referencing. Heritage ensures that the curriculum is research-based with over 80 references from widely accepted social science research to support curriculum information. The Heritage Keepers curricula have long been approved by the National Abstinence Clearinghouse for adherence to federal A-H legislative requirements for abstinence education as set forth in Section 510(b) of Title V of the Social Security Act. The Heritage Keepers program also meets all 66 standards of the CDC [Centers for Disease Control and Prevention]–funded SMARTool (Systematic Method for Assessing Risk-avoidance Tool).

Unfortunately, organizations that strive to help young people "develop a strong sense of personal identity and worth, set protective boundaries, resist negative peer pressure, determine and protect personal values and goals, and set high standards" are just too darn conservative for organizations such as the ACLU; regardless of research showing the program helps keep youth free of STDs and unwanted pregnancies, organizations like Heritage are on the wrong side of the political fence.

> **FAST FACT**
>
> A 2011 Centers for Disease Control and Prevention report on condom use by teens and the incidence of STDs in this same population found that while reported condom use by teens has increased, so has the prevalence of STDs, suggesting that an emphasis on condoms in sex education does not necessarily lead to a decrease in STDs.

Abstinence and Restraint Are Not Just Conservative Values

The Philadelphia School District, as evidenced by the fact that they are pushing condoms while refusing to promote values such as abstinence and restraint, has voiced its position loud and clear. *Who needs conservative restraint when we have the progressive convenience of condoms?*

Again, this is unfortunate. Abstinence and restraint are life skills that transcend politics—rise above race, gender, religion, and sexual orientation. As Thanissaro Bhikkhu, a Buddhist abbot, published author, and noted scholar on Eastern philosophy wrote in his essay "The Dignity of Restraint":

> What's good about it? Well, for one thing, if we don't have any restraint, we don't have any control over where our lives are going. Anything that comes our way immediately pulls us into

its wake. We don't have any strong sense of priorities, of what's really worthwhile, of what's not worthwhile, of the pleasures we'd gain by saying no to other pleasures. How do we rank the pleasures in our lives, the happiness, the sense of well-being that we get in various ways? Actually, there's a sense of well-being that comes from being totally independent, from not needing other things. If that state of well-being doesn't have a chance to develop, if we're constantly giving in to our impulse to do this or take that, we'll never know what that well-being is.

At the same time, we'll never know our impulses. When you simply ride with your impulses, you don't understand their force. They're like the currents below the surface of a river: only if you

Philadelphia mayor Michael Nutter has come under criticism from abstinence-only advocates for his program of placing condoms in high schools.

try to build a dam across the river will you detect those currents and appreciate how strong they are. So we have to look at what's important in life, develop a strong sense of priorities, and be willing to say no to the currents that would lead to less worthwhile pleasures. . . .

It's important that we realize the role that restraint plays in overcoming the problem of suffering and finding true well-being for ourselves. You realize that you're not giving up anything you really need. You're a lot better off without it. There's a part of the mind that resists this truth, and our culture hasn't been very helpful at all because it encourages that resistance: "Give in to this impulse, give in to that impulse, obey your thirst. It's good for the economy, it's good for you spiritually. Watch out, if you repress your desires you're going to get tied up in psychological knots." The lessons our culture teaches us—to go out and buy, buy, buy; be greedy, be greedy; give in, give in—are all over the place. And what kind of dignity comes from following those messages? The dignity of a fish gobbling down bait. We've got to unlearn those habits, unlearn those messages, if we want to revive words like *dignity* and *restraint*, and to reap the rewards that the realities of dignity and restraint have to offer our minds.

EVALUATING THE AUTHOR'S ARGUMENTS:

Viewpoint author Christopher Paslay believes that abstinence and restraint should be taught in sex education classes alongside other values. Do you agree with the author that these values should be taught in school? Do you think that students will just do what they want anyway? Are these values political? Explain your answers.

Virginity Pledges Work for Some Teens

> "We should make virginity pledges available for those young people who sincerely wish to make a commitment to abstinence."

Steven Martino

In the viewpoint that follows Steven Martino argues that contrary to recent studies, his own study done for the Rand Corporation, a respected research institute, shows that virginity pledges can and do work for some teens. Martino contends that although these pledges may not be for every teen, teens that pledge to remain virgins, especially younger teens, seem to remain virgins for longer than those who do not take these pledges. The study done by Rand surveyed young people between the ages of twelve and seventeen and found that teens who took the pledges remained virgins longer than those who did not. Martino concludes that this means that pledged teens are less likely to contract sexually transmitted diseases.

Martino holds a doctorate in psychology and is a behavioral scientist at the Rand Corporation.

AS YOU READ, CONSIDER THE FOLLOWING QUESTIONS:

1. Why, in the author's view, is it important for teens to delay the start of sexual activity?
2. What does the author say the Rand study found after following for three years young people who took a virginity pledge and those who did not?
3. Martino says that knowing that virginity pledges work to delay sex for some teens, it is prudent that sex education programs do what?

Over the past decade, millions of teens in the United States have made formal pledges to delay sex until they are married. Virginity pledges are part of a wider abstinence movement that has been a controversial approach to sex education.

Essentially, the available research suggests that teaching abstinence alone to teenagers does not work—they are no more likely to delay the start of sexual activity than other teenagers. But research has not been so clear regarding virginity pledges specifically.

Some studies have found that pledges may help young people delay the start of sexual activity. This would be important regardless of one's religious or moral stance on sexual activity, because we know that delaying the start of sex reduces a teenager's risk of an unintended pregnancy and contracting a sexually transmitted disease.

The latest study on the issue, published in the January issue of the journal *Pediatrics*, seems to throw cold water on the idea that virginity pledges do much good, finding no difference in sexual activity between pledgers and nonpledgers. Those findings appear to be in direct conflict with those of a similar study I led at the RAND

FAST FACT

Studies suggest that virginity pledges do encourage students who hold strong religious beliefs to abstain from sex, as well as their gaining a sense of being unique because they are the only ones among their peers who take the pledge.

Corporation, published last summer in the Journal of Adolescent Health.

So which study is right? The truth is that pledges seem to delay sex for some kids some of the time.

Virginity pledges do not work in the strictest sense of delaying sex until marriage. Almost everyone has sex before they are married (95 percent of Americans), and that includes those who take virginity pledges.

That pledges fail is understandable. Teens' relationship circumstances change. Their perspectives may change. What matters is that at the time young people take a virginity pledge, they express a desire to delay sex. Taking a virginity pledge may help them to do so.

So, who are the "some kids" for whom virginity pledges seem to work? They seem to be most (perhaps solely) effective among younger teens. The new *Pediatrics* study investigated the effectiveness of pledges taken at age 16 or older. In contrast, the RAND study focused on pledges taken between the ages of 12 and 17, or earlier.

Pledges also seem to work for only a limited period, or stage of life. The RAND study followed youth for 3 years until they were 15 to

A Rand Corporation study shows that virginity pledges do work for teens who have strong religious backgrounds and less-positive attitudes toward sex, as well as having parents that keep close track of them.

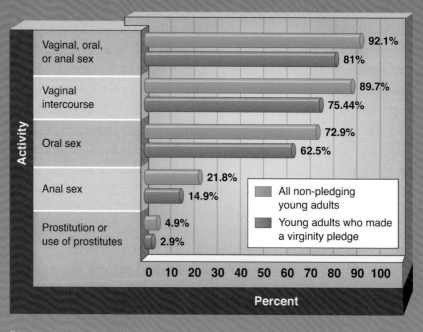

Sexual Activity and Risk Behaviors of Young Adults Who Did and Did Not Take a Virginity Pledge

Activity

Vaginal, oral, or anal sex — 92.1% / 81%

Vaginal intercourse — 89.7% / 75.44%

Oral sex — 72.9% / 62.5%

Anal sex — 21.8% / 14.9%

Prostitution or use of prostitutes — 4.9% / 2.9%

All non-pledging young adults

Young adults who made a virginity pledge

0 10 20 30 40 50 60 70 80 90 100

Percent

Taken from: National Longitude Study of Adolescent Health. Robert Rector and Kurt A. Johnson. "Adolescent Virginity Pledges and Risky Sexual Behavior," Heritage Foundation, June 14, 2005. www.heritage.org.

20 years old, and found that 42 percent of pledgers remained virgins, while only 33 percent of similar nonpledgers did so.

The new *Pediatrics* study followed participants for five years after they reported having taken a pledge, until they were 20 or older, and found that they typically had sex for the first time at age 21. By that time, pledgers and nonpledgers appear equally likely to have had sex. If the pledge delays sex until after the teen years, rather than until marriage, there would still be significant health benefits.

With this knowledge, the most prudent course of action is to offer virginity pledges as part of a comprehensive program of sex education that includes information on birth control methods and condoms.

After all, most young people do not take virginity pledges, and most (65 percent of boys and 70 percent of girls) have sex as teenagers. Even many virginity pledgers will have sex as teenagers, and they need to know how to protect themselves from unintended pregnancy and sexually transmitted diseases when they do.

Should all kids pledge? The answer is clearly "no." The RAND study showed that pledges work for teens with strong religious backgrounds and less positive attitudes toward sex, and who have parents that keep close track of them. Other work indicates pledges must be freely undertaken and that pledges are ineffective if all kids in a school or community take them.

Instead, we should make virginity pledges available for those young people who sincerely wish to make a commitment to abstinence, and provide all young people with the education and skills they need to protect themselves from unintended pregnancy, sexually transmitted diseases, and emotional harm once they do become sexually active.

EVALUATING THE AUTHOR'S ARGUMENTS:

After reading viewpoint author Steven Martino's evidence about the effectiveness of virginity pledges in delaying sexual activity in teens, do you agree with his viewpoint? Do you think sex education programs should focus on other ways to reduce the spread of STDs? Why do you think one type of program is more effective than the other? Explain your answer using facts from the articles.

Virginity Pledges Do Not Help Reduce the Spread of STDs

Dudley Barlow

Dudley Barlow, a retired high school English teacher, argues in the following viewpoint that the virginity pledges that accompany abstinence-only education fail in their goal of convincing teens to abstain from sex until marriage. He presents evidence from various studies that have found abstinence-only education at best leads to the same outcomes in teen sexual behavior as no sex education or other methods of instruction and at worst leads teens to engage in less-safe sex than other forms of education. Barlow worries that the attachment of federal funds to abstinence-only education was a mistake and should be repealed, allowing educators to find a middle ground where abstinence is promoted alongside contraception and details about reproduction.

"Abstinence programs may not affect sexual behavior, but may increase unsafe sex."

Dudley Barlow, "The Teachers' Lounge: Sex Ed. Redux, Redux, Redux," *Education Digest*, February 2009. Republished with permission.

AS YOU READ, CONSIDER THE FOLLOWING QUESTIONS:

1. In the article by Janet Elise Rosenbaum, as cited by the author, what did virginity pledgers report five years after making the pledge?
2. What was the impact of sex-ed programs on teenagers' sexual behavior three to seventeen months after the end of the program, according to the report by Debra Hauser cited by Barlow?
3. As stated by the author, how much money does the federal government spend on abstinence programs?

Some years ago, I saw a TV news story about an adolescent girl—in Texas, as I recall—taking a virginity pledge. Could it have been Shelby Knox, the girl who, when she became alarmed about the number of pregnant girls she saw in her high school, changed from being an abstinence only adherent to a sex education reformer? In this ceremony, her father placed a purity ring on her ring finger, and she promised him that she would remain chaste until she married. I thought it was unsettling—creepy really—that in a ceremony emulating a wedding, she would pledge her troth to her dad. If she had premarital sex, it would signal her betrayal of her father? It sounded a little incestuous to me.

Abstinence Programs Could Increase Unsafe Sex

And now, as it turns out, we have more substantive reasons to question the value of teenagers taking virginity pledges. They don't work. Harvard researcher Janet Elise Rosenbaum reported on February 13, 2008, in a paper titled "Patient teenagers?: A Comparison of the Sexual Behavior of Virginity Pledgers and Matched Non-pledgers" that "Virginity pledgers and closely-matched non-pledgers have virtually identical sexual behavior, but pledgers are less likely to protect themselves from pregnancy and disease before marriage than matched non-pledgers. Abstinence programs may not affect sexual behavior, but may increase unsafe sex."

In the January 2009 issue of the journal *Pediatrics,* Rosenbaum reported the results of a five-year longitudinal study she conducted on a nationally representative sample of middle and high school students to compare the sexual behavior of students who had taken virginity pledges to the sexual behavior of students who had not taken such pledges.

The results of this study confirmed what she wrote in her February paper. Not only did pledgers and non-pledgers not differ in premarital sex, they had the same incidence and types of sexually transmitted diseases. Pledgers reported 0.1 fewer past-year partners, but did not differ in lifetime sexual partners or the age at which they first had sex. Rosenbaum also reports, curiously enough, that five years after they made virginity pledges, 84% of the pledgers denied ever having pledged.

Federal Funds Tied to Abstinence-Only Education

In "Five Years of Abstinence-Only-Until-Marriage Education: Assessing the Impact" Debra Hauser, vice president of Advocates for Youth, reports that: "In 1996, Congress signed into law the Personal Responsibility & Work Opportunities Reconciliation Act, or 'welfare reform.' Attached was the provision, later set out in Section 510(b) of Title V of the Social Security Act, appropriating $250 million [. . .] over five years for state initiatives promoting sexual abstinence outside of marriage as the only acceptable standard of behavior for young people."

The important point here, of course, is that Title V denies federal funding to any sex education program that does not promote sexual abstinence outside of marriage as the only acceptable standard of behavior for young people. Comprehensive sex education programs: "Education that promotes abstinence but includes information about contraception and condoms to build young people's knowledge, attitudes and skills for when they do become sexually active," are not eligible for federal funds.

FAST FACT

Students who take virginity pledges are as likely as students who have not taken pledges to have a sexually transmitted disease (STD), according to research published in the *Journal of Adolescent Health*. Additionally, the research found that students who had taken the pledge sought testing and treatment for STDs in smaller numbers than those who had not taken the pledge.

"For the first five years of the initiative," Hauser reports, "every state but California participated in the program. (California had experimented with its own abstinence-only initiative in the early 1990s. The program was terminated in February 1996, when evaluation results found the program to be ineffective.) From 1998 to 2003, almost a half a billion dollars in state and federal funds were appropriated to support the Title V initiative. A report, detailing the results from the federally funded evaluation of select Title V programs, was due to be released more than a year ago. Last year [2008], Congress extended 'welfare reform' and, with it, the Title V abstinence-only-until-marriage funding without benefit of this, as yet unreleased, report."

Teens' Attitudes Toward Sex Are Not Affected by Any Education Program Long Term

Even though the report on federally funded Title V programs has not been issued, Advocates for Youth did manage to identify evaluations from 10 states. These evaluations measured three things: attitudes endorsing abstinence, intentions to abstain, and actual sexual behavior.

Four of 10 programs showed increases in attitudes favorable to abstinence. Three of 10 showed mixed results, and 3 had no significant impact on attitudes.

Three of 9 programs showed a favorable impact on intentions to abstain. Two of 9 showed mixed results, and 4 of 9 showed no significant impact on participants' intentions to abstain.

Finally, 1 of 6 programs showed mixed results in changes in sexual behavior. Three of 6 programs showed no impact, and 2 of 6 programs actually reported increases in sexual behavior. Possible causes of the increased sexual behavior were unclear.

"Two evaluations," Hauser writes,

Iowa's and the Pennsylvania Fulton County program—compared the impact of comprehensive sex education with that of abstinence-only-until-marriage programs.

In Iowa, abstinence-only students were slightly more likely than comprehensive sex education participants to feel strongly about wanting to postpone sex, but less likely to feel that their goals should not include teen pregnancy. There was little to no difference between the abstinence-only students and those in the comprehensive sex education program in understanding of why they should wait to have sex. Evaluations did not include comparison of data on the sexual behavior of participants in the two types of programs.

In Fulton County, PA, results found few to no differences between the abstinence-only and comprehensive approaches in attitudes towards sexual behavior. Evaluators found that, regardless of which program was implemented in the 7th and 8th grades, sexual attitudes, intentions, and behaviors were similar by the end of the 10th grade.

But the bottom line is this: "No evaluation demonstrated any impact on reducing teens' sexual behavior at follow-up, 3 to 17 months after the program ended."

Abstinence-Only Programs Do Not Provide Students with Important Information

Finally, Hauser reports that the results of these surveys are consistent with other studies that have been done on the efficacy of abstinence-only sex education. She cites the work of researcher Doug Kirby. "In a 1994 review of sex education programs, Kirby et al. assessed all the studies available at the time of school-based, abstinence-only programs that had received peer review and that measured attitudes, intentions, and behavior. Kirby et al. found that none of the three abstinence-only programs was effective in producing a statistically significant impact on sexual behaviors in program participants relative to comparisons. In a 1997 report for the National Campaign to Prevent Teen Pregnancy, . . . Kirby reviewed evaluations from six abstinence-only programs, again finding no program that produced a statistically significant change in sexual behavior. This was again confirmed in 2000, when another review by Kirby found no abstinence-only program that produced statistically significant changes in sexual behaviors among program youth relative to comparisons."

Hauser also writes that a few of the evaluators of the 10 state programs were concerned that abstinence-only programs failed to address the needs of the significant number of sexually active youth.

The concerned evaluators remarked that abstinence-only programs failed to provide youth with information they needed to protect themselves from pregnancy and sexually transmitted diseases.

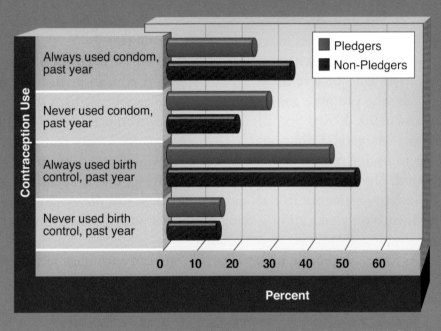

Use of Contraception by Teens, Grades Seven to Twelve, Who Either Took or Did Not Take a Virginity Pledge

Contraception Use

- Always used condom, past year
- Never used condom, past year
- Always used birth control, past year
- Never used birth control, past year

Legend: Pledgers / Non-Pledgers

X-axis: 0 10 20 30 40 50 60

Percent

Taken from: Janet Elise Rosenbaum. "Patient Teenagers? A Comparison of the Sexual Behavior of Virginity Pledgers and Matched Nonpledgers." *Pediatrics*, vol. 123, no. 1, January 1, 2009. Chart on www.epiphenom.fieldofscience.com.

Ironically, abstinence-only programs may actually increase these risks for sexually active teens. Hauser writes, "Evaluators noted more than once that the programs' emphasis on the failure rates of contraception, including condoms, left youth ambivalent, at best, about using them." One wonders whether an underlying premise of abstinence-only programs is that sexually active youth are beyond the pale and are, therefore, on their own.

Brian DeVries, of the National Sexuality Resource Center, says, "We want people to know that abstinence-only education doesn't work. Sex educators know. Teens know. Parents know. And the research shows it. When will our policies and interventions reflect what science, research, and best practices demonstrate? We need comprehensive sexuality education that is truly comprehensive."

A Middle Ground on Sex Education Is Needed

The federal government spends about $200 million annually on abstinence programs that are demonstrably ineffective, but it is difficult to imagine that members of Congress will be in a hurry to curtail funding for these programs. Who among them (particularly members from conservative areas of the country) is likely to risk being labeled as someone who wants to encourage premarital sex?

So, are we stuck with this impassable divide between social conservatives who believe in abstinence-only sex education and social liberals who promote comprehensive sex education? Perhaps not. In an article titled "Red Sex, Blue Sex" in the November 3, 2008, *New Yorker*, Margaret Talbot holds out some hope for a view that might help to bridge this divide. She says Shelby Knox "occupies a middle ground. She testified [at a congressional hearing] that it's possible to 'believe in abstinence in a religious sense,' but still understand that abstinence-only education is dangerous for students who simply are not abstaining.

"As Knox's approach, makes clear, . . . you can encourage teenagers to postpone sex for all kinds of practical, emotional, and moral reasons. A new 'abstinence-plus' curriculum, now growing in popularity, urges abstinence while providing accurate information about contraception and reproduction for those who have sex anyway. 'Abstinence works,' Knox said. 'Abstinence-only-until-marriage does not.'"

EVALUATING THE AUTHOR'S ARGUMENTS:

After reading all of the chapter's viewpoints about the impact of education on teens' sexual behavior, including comprehensive versus abstinence-only education, providing condoms in schools, and virginity pledges, which method do you think is most effective? Why? Have you experienced any of these methods in your school? How did you and your friends feel about them, and how, if at all, did they affect your behavior?

Chapter 3

Would Government Regulation Reduce STD Infection Rates?

Many home STD-testing kits are now on the market.

Viewpoint

1

Mandatory STD Testing Would Reduce Infection Rates

Rosa Freedman

"Mandatory [STD] testing would enable people to stop infecting others without realising it."

In the viewpoint that follows Rosa Freedman argues that mandatory STD testing in the United Kingdom (UK) would reduce the STD infection rates in that country. She contends that currently, individuals experience no benefit from knowing they carry an STD, and if they do know, they must pay high health care premiums. Further, Freedman states, by remaining unaware of their STD status, people can claim ignorance if they infect another person and avoid suffering any penalty. The author argues that by making testing mandatory, insurance companies could no longer discriminate against STD carriers, the law would punish those who knowingly spread disease, and individuals without STDs would have the ability to make informed decisions about the risks associated with certain sexual partners.

Freedman is a human rights researcher at Queen Mary University in London and a contributor to the *Guardian*, a major British newspaper.

AS YOU READ, CONSIDER THE FOLLOWING QUESTIONS:
1. According to the author, how many UK individuals were diagnosed with chlamydia in 2008?
2. Under what act does Freedman state that individuals can be charged for failing to disclose their STD to their sex partners?
3. When, in the author's opinion, could the mandatory STD tests be administered?

W̲e all know the risks of unprotected sex, thanks to public education campaigns. And there have also been efforts to encourage people to seek an STD [sexually transmitted disease] test, notably for chlamydia, which can cause infertility: another 200,000 people were diagnosed with it in the UK [United Kingdom] in 2008. Yet important elements in our society seem to encourage people not to find out whether they have an STD. Their sexual partners, meanwhile, would prefer not to contemplate it. So STDs are transmitted to people who have not had the opportunity to consent to that risk of infection. Draconian [harsh] as it may sound, the only way around this might be mandatory testing for STDs.

FAST FACT

The American Social Health Association estimates that less than half of all adults aged eighteen to forty-four have been tested for an STD other than HIV in their lifetime.

Individuals Have No Incentive to Get Tested for STDs

Private medical coverage has become widespread, and companies often encourage members to improve their health, such as by using a gym regularly, through discounts on their premiums. Yet those same companies are effectively discouraging STD testing by the way they treat potential customers who have been infected. Health insurance is particularly difficult to obtain for those with HIV. Premiums may be greatly increased for those with other STDs. A person who has engaged in risky behaviour is incentivised [motivated] not to discover his or her status for fear of falling foul of these companies.

Criminal law offers similar disincentives. A person may be prosecuted if, knowing they have a disease, they engage in unprotected sexual intercourse and infect his or her partner. Prosecution will depend on whether the other party was told of the STD before intercourse took place, giving them the choice to consent to risk of infection. Failure

A British billboard advertises free STD testing. Proponents of mandatory STD testing say it would reduce the rate of infection.

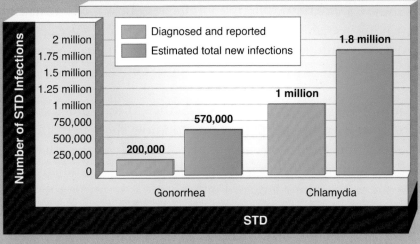

Many Youths Are Unaware of Their STD Infections

Number of STD Infections

- Diagnosed and reported
- Estimated total new infections

Gonorrhea: 200,000 / 570,000

Chlamydia: 1 million / 1.8 million

Y-axis: 0, 250,000, 500,000, 750,000, 1 million, 1.25 million, 1.5 million, 1.75 million, 2 million

X-axis: STD

Note: Data is for individuals age fifteen to twenty-four.

Taken from: Centers for Disease Control and Prevention. *Sexually Transmitted Infections Among Young Americans,* 2013.

to disclose may result in a charge under the Offences Against the Person Act 1861. Spreading diseases requires heavy sentencing, for both deterrent and punitive reasons. Criminal law becomes asinine where it deals with diseases spread by a person ignorant of his or her status. Such persons can defend a charge on the basis that lack of knowledge negates the duty to disclose.

Mandatory STD Testing Would Make Everyone Healthier

In the event of an epidemic, various methods are used to contain the threat and prevent its spread. Isolation, mandatory treatment and other measures may be introduced. The spread of sexually transmitted diseases—including HIV, which is again on the rise in England—can be classed as an epidemic. Mandatory testing, knowledge of status and the legal incentive to pass on that information, would limit that spread. Tests could be carried out at annual GP [general practitioner] check-ups, or when a person seeks other medical treatment from doctors or in hospitals, and the results kept on their confidential NHS [National Health Service] records.

Mandatory testing would not necessarily mean that STD carriers cannot engage in unprotected sex. It would result in carriers knowing their status, and requiring them to tell the other person of, and obtain their consent to, the risk of infection. Informed consent may allow unprotected sex depending on the STD's classification under the different criminal "harms", as serious diseases like HIV cannot be consented to under current law. Criminal convictions would deter failure to disclose, and punish those ignoring that duty.

An individual's right to decide whether to find out their status is trumped by other people's rights to know the risk of infection. Would compulsory tests be unpopular? Probably. But while insurers continue to discriminate against people with STDs, and advertising and educational campaigns will only go so far in preventing further infections, mandatory testing would enable people to stop infecting others without realising it.

EVALUATING THE AUTHOR'S ARGUMENTS:

The author of this viewpoint, Rosa Freedman, argues for mandatory STD testing in the United Kingdom. After reading why she believes these tests should be done, do you believe that a similar plan could be put into place in the United States? Do you see any differences between the current laws or circumstances in the two countries that would make such testing in the United States more difficult or unpopular? Explain.

Removing the Stigma Attached to STDs Would Reduce Infection Rates

"The worst part of having herpes is being subject to the stigma of a society [that] treats a simple skin infection like a death sentence."

Emily McCombs

Emily McCombs argues in the following viewpoint that making villains out of the people who infect others with sexually transmitted diseases (STDs), especially non-life-threatening ones, only discourages those people from getting tested and sharing that knowledge with their sexual partners. McCombs asserts that most people who pass STDs on to their partners are unaware that they are even infected. To combat this problem, the author believes that society should work to counter the notion that those who have STDs are monsters. In her opinion, this would allow everyone to feel less embarrassed about getting tested, finding out they have an STD, and informing their future partners about their status, which in turn could reduce infection rates.

Emily McCombs, "In Defense of People Who Give You Herpes," *xoJane*, June 6, 2012. www.xojane.com. Reprinted with permission of Say Media, Inc.

McCombs is the executive editor of *xoJane,* an online magazine, and has contributed to a wide range of online and print publications.

AS YOU READ, CONSIDER THE FOLLOWING QUESTIONS:
1. According to the author, what percentage of people who have HSV-2 have never received an official diagnosis of the disease?
2. What STD is not screened for in a standard STD test, according to McCombs?
3. The author states that even people who know they have herpes and infect other people are not evil but what?

Nobody wants an STD. (I know that's kind of a sweeping statement, but I feel pretty good about it.) I guess that's why, when it comes to the topic of getting one, or especially the dirty screwed-up sociopaths who give them to people, emotions run high. And why a few times a year, one of these STD vigilante stories pop up, like this chick who posted fliers of a one-night stand who allegedly gave her the herp, this other guy who did the same weird flyer thing and the Oregon woman who was just awarded 900,000 dollars after suing the man who gave her herpes.

The story goes like this: A 49-year-old woman met a 69-year-old man on an Internet dating site. The woman says that she asked her date to wear a condom and he agreed, but when they were actually having sex she realized that he had not put on a condom. Afterward, he told her he had herpes.

I also really like this line from [Portland's *Oregonian* newspaper website] Oregon Live: "The woman was looking for a husband. Instead, she ended up with genital herpes." You can have both, you know!

The man, for his part says that he didn't think the disease was transmittable because he wasn't having an outbreak, and that he told her after

> **FAST FACT**
>
> According to the American Social Health Association, it costs in excess of $8 billion to address the STD problem in the United States, including both diagnosis and treatment.

they had sex because he liked her and wanted her to know that there might be times when they would have to refrain from sex. And look, that may be dumb, but it's not an uncommon kind of dumb. There's a lot of misinformation out there about STDs, even very common ones like HSV [herpes simplex virus] and HPV [human papillomavirus].

You know why there's so much misinformation? Because of the extreme stigma surrounding these widespread infections that keep us from openly discussing them.

Most People Are Unaware They Have an STD

And in this specific case, the guy knew he had herpes. But he is the exception, not the rule. In all the media hand-wringing about who gave the creepie crawlies to whom, what almost always gets left out is that most, *most* infected people do not know they carry the virus. Like, 75% to 90% of people who test positive for HSV-2 have never been officially diagnosed with genital herpes. One study at an STD clinic found that 60 percent of infected women never had any symptoms.

This patient suffers from herpes, which is sexually transmitted. The standard STD test does not include herpes so a person needs to get a test specifically for herpes to find out whether the virus is present.

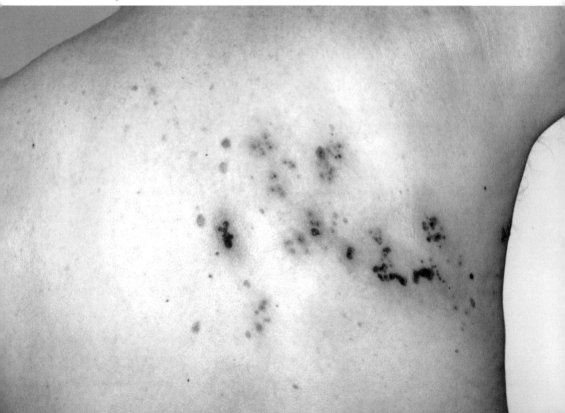

There is a blood test that can test for the presence of HSV-2 without outbreaks, but a standard STD test does not screen for herpes. If you've never had an outbreak, or specifically asked to be blood-tested for herpes, you probably haven't been tested. So, in the words of MTV's *Diary*, "You think you know but you have no idea."

And it's mostly these asymptomatic people who are passing on the virus, not the STD boogie monsters out there willy nilly spreading their cooties as wantonly as they must have spread their legs to get their stupid whore disease. Don't believe me? Believe science! According to [a] study in the *Journal of the American Medical Association*, "Most HSV-2 infections are acquired from persons without a clinical history of genital herpes." So before you judge someone else, how sure are you of your own status?

Let me repeat that again, because it's important: Most people who infect other people with herpes are doing so unknowingly.

Open Discussion of STDs Should Be Encouraged

To illustrate the point, I received this letter recently in response to a post we ran about herpes several months ago:

> I was married for 20 years. When I got a divorce, I went and had the whole panel of tests, so I could say I had papers. When I came back positive for herpes, I was floored. I cannot recall ever having an outbreak. I called the ex. He said all his tests were negative! I called the OB [obstetrician] who delivered the kids. She said they didn't test for that back then. I called the kids' pediatrician. He said it was really common among women my age (47) to find out this way. This year my gynecologist says I am probably a dormant carrier (and have been for more than 22 years)! Who knew?

It's stories like this woman's that are much more common than the scare stories we're always hearing about. Maybe it makes us feel safer to rail against the evil person we imagine intentionally inflicting us with the Scarlet H [for herpes, analogous to the letter A worn by Hester Prynne in *The Scarlet Letter*]. But what would actually make us all safer is if we all went and asked our doctors for blood tests, even if we have always had smug, blemish-free vaginas.

And if we reduced stigma, so that those who do know they're carrying the herpes virus aren't too scared and ashamed to tell you about it. Because even people who knowingly expose others to herpes aren't evil people; they're scared ones. And considering that herpes doesn't kill you, or even necessarily harm you, in the case of the huge amount of people who are asymptomatic or only ever have one outbreak, they shouldn't have to be.

I don't mean to defend this particular guy so much as to point out that the cultural narrative represented by his story is a misleading one. There is not a legion of soulless herpes monsters out to deliberately wreck your once-pristine genitals, and acting as if there are doesn't encourage anyone to be forthright about their status.

I don't begrudge this woman the $900,000 paycheck she'll receive for both contracting the disease and the resultant anxiety and depression. As many of the commenters pointed out, the "I'm wearing a condom/not really" move doesn't exactly inspire sympathy for the defendant.

But for a lot of people, the worst part of having herpes is being subject to the stigma of a society [that] treats a simple skin infection like a death sentence.

EVALUATING THE AUTHOR'S ARGUMENTS:

Consider viewpoint author Emily McCombs's argument that the stigma from STDs should be removed in light of Rosa Freedman's opinion in the previous viewpoint that STD testing should be mandatory. Do you think that mandatory testing would help to remove this stigma or increase it? Use evidence from the viewpoints to support your claims.

Governments Should Mandate the HPV Vaccine

Amanda Marcotte

"The only real way to protect the populace against disease is mandating vaccinations."

Much debate in recent years has surrounded when and whether to vaccinate young women for the human papillomavirus (HPV). Amanda Marcotte argues in the following viewpoint that the HPV vaccine should be mandatory for all young girls because it is the only way to ensure that women will not contract this potentially life-threatening disease. A mandate, in the author's opinion, would ensure that people would not have to individually determine whether the benefits of getting the vaccine outweigh the risks of not getting it, and they would eventually accept the law and stop worrying about their unwarranted fears. These fears, Marcotte contends, result only from right-wing fear mongering and should not be seriously considered when making a decision that could impact one's health.

Marcotte is an American liberal blogger who writes about feminism and politics.

AS YOU READ, CONSIDER THE FOLLOWING QUESTIONS:
  1. What misinformation does Marcotte claim liberals have "heard from somewhere" about the HPV vaccine?
  2. What characteristics of HPV lead the author to state that a vaccine for it "really should be mandated"?
  3. As stated by the author, what has history shown about vaccinations?

Laura Bassett at the Huffington Post has an excellent, must-read rundown of the whole controversy over the HPV vaccine that's been stirred up with Michele Bachmann's ignorant statements about it. I wish everyone would read this; it addresses much of the confusion that has leaked into the public because the abstinence-only fanatics have been studiously spreading misinformation. I've been alarmed at how many liberals I've spoken to, online and off, who heard from somewhere that the vaccine is "untested" and that it's somehow less safe than every other vaccine on the market. In reality,

The viewpoint author contends that HPV vaccination should be mandatory for all young girls because it is the only way to ensure that they will not contract this potentially life-threatening disease.

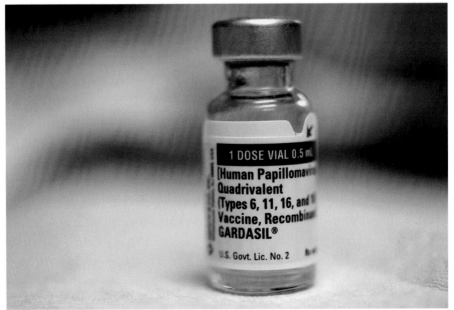

it's been shown to be, both in medical tests and in the information gathered from widespread vaccination, that it's as safe as other vaccines. That's the power that the rumor mill can have when it comes to things like this; it can create unease in people who may balk at a more blatant argument that you deserve to get HPV if you aren't a virgin who marries a virgin (and that apparently means a "kissing" virgin as well).

The most damage that the right wing rumor mill has done to the HPV vaccine is they've managed to convince people, even liberals, that the vaccine is somehow a ceremonial introduction to adult sexuality. But from what I understand, the rationale for giving it to 6th graders was that it's a young enough age that it doesn't have to be that. (There's also some medical reasons that involve maximizing the effectiveness of it.) We're still in the habit in this country of thinking that sexual health care and self-awareness should start *after* sexual initiation, especially for women. It's getting better than it used to be in many ways; for instance, the notion that virgins can't use tampons, which was widespread when I was young, seems to have declined significantly. It also used to be typical for teenagers to lose their virginity and *then* start considering their contraceptive strategy, but now the majority of teenagers use some kind of contraception the first time they have sex. Conservative fears that virgins familiarizing themselves with contraception and having condoms on themselves in case they want to have sex would increase the rate of teenage sexual activity have been proven completely wrong. The Guttmacher Institute has demonstrated that kids are actually waiting longer for sex than they did in the past. I suspect that sending the message that sex is something you plan for, instead of something that you do spontaneously and then deal with, probably influences the decision to wait longer.

FAST FACT

The federal Advisory Committee on Immunization Practices (ACIP) suggested in 2006 that all females be vaccinated for the human papillomavirus (HPV) and then later, in 2011, the ACIP advised that all males also be vaccinated for HPV.

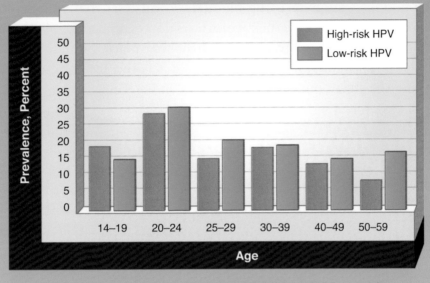

High-Risk and Low-Risk Types of HPV Among Females Age Fourteen to Fifty-Nine in the United States, 2003–2004

Taken from: National Health and Nutrition Examination Survey. *JAMA*, 2007. American Medical Association. On Center for Disease Controland Prevention. *2008 Sexually Transmitted Diseases Surveillance*, 2008.

Because HPV is widespread, nearly inevitable if you're not vaccinated, and has the potential to create medical problems or even kill you, it really should be mandated. I prefer as a rule to err on the side of freedom, but when it comes to public health issues, the government often has to get involved. Human beings struggle to weigh the risks and benefits of certain choices already—which is why we have lung cancer, unintended pregnancy, and nutrition-related diseases—and it only gets worse when you introduce the argument that you should participate in a behavior for the common good as well as your own. That's why we have laws against drunk driving and speeding, because people foolishly tend to think of their driving choices as an individual issue, instead of a common good one. Same with vaccinations. History has shown that people overrate the dangers of getting them, underrate the dangers of not getting them, and blow off their responsibilities not to spread disease (or at least have blanched at the idea that they should suffer a minor pinprick in order to help establish herd immunity). Unfortunately, the only real way to protect the populace against disease is mandating vaccinations, because human nature is flawed in such a way that voluntary vaccinations just don't cut it. History also shows that, by and large, the populace stops resisting mandates soon after they're put into place, probably because their worst fears don't come to pass and they simply forget they were worried in the first place. So it should be with HPV. Mandating it will result in a negative result of nothing, taking the steam out of right wing fear-mongering.

EVALUATING THE AUTHOR'S ARGUMENTS:

After reading Amanda Marcotte's viewpoint that explains that mandatory vaccination is the only way to ensure an entire population is safe from a disease, what is your opinion on mandatory HPV vaccination? Do you believe that all young girls should be required to get the vaccine even if they will not be personally at risk for becoming infected with the disease? Is vaccinating for the greater good more important than individual beliefs? Explain your answer.

Legalizing Prostitution Would Reduce the Spread of STDs

Alison Bass

"Legalizing sex work actually reduces the spread of sexually transmitted diseases."

Alison Bass, an award-winning journalist who writes about prostitution and the author of the book *Side Effects*, argues in the following viewpoint that Canada's proactive approach to prostitution should be emulated in the United States because it protects sex workers and encourages those involved to practice safe sex, which will reduce the spread of STDs. In addition to the Canadian example, she points to studies done in the Netherlands, where prostitution is legal, to show that legalizing prostitution effectively combats the problems that exist in the sex trade. Bass concludes that the benefits of legalization evidenced from these examples include protecting sex workers from violence, limiting the public's exposure to STDs, and reducing the prevalence of underage prostitution.

AS YOU READ, CONSIDER THE FOLLOWING QUESTIONS:
1. According to the author, a federal appeals court in Canada over-turned laws against prostitution in Ontario arguing that crimi-nalizing prostitution did what?
2. The Canadian appeals court based its ruling on new research showing what negative effects of laws against prostitution, according to Bass?
3. Bass cites a study from the Netherlands, done seven years after prostitution was legalized in that country, that found that legal-izing prostitution resulted in what benefits?

Just as Canada has provided us with a model for affordable health care, our neighbors to the north may also be leading the way on another key issue: reducing the spread of AIDS and other sexually transmitting diseases.

A few months ago [in March 2012], a federal appeals court in Canada overturned laws against prostitution in the province of Ontario, argu-ing that criminalizing sex work increased the risks of violence against women and made it harder for them to practice safe sex.

The federal government is appealing the ruling, which essentially legalizes brothels in Ontario and allows prostitutes to hire bodyguards. Legal observers say the Supreme Court of Canada could take up the case as early as this fall [the high court upheld the ruling in late 2013, thus legalizing prostitution in Canada].

Research Supports the Legalization of Prostitution

The court based its ruling on new research showing that laws against prostitution actually increase the likelihood of physical and sexual violence against sex workers and the chance they may spread sexually transmitted diseases like AIDS. For example, one study published in *Social Science and Medicine* last year [2011] found that criminalizing indoors sex work forced Canadian women to sell sex on the streets, making it more difficult for them to refuse clients who didn't want to wear condoms (which can prevent the spread of disease).

Likewise, another study published in the *British Medical Journal* in 2009 found that of 237 street walkers in British Columbia who were forced to sell sex outdoors (because they couldn't see clients at their residences), more than half (57 per cent) experienced physical or sexual violence in an 18-month period.

As Dr. Kate Shannon, lead author of the study and a researcher at the British Columbia Centre for Excellence in HIV/AIDS, said: "These women continue to be pushed to work in isolated spaces, with limited access to housing and drug treatment which further compounds their risk of being physically assaulted or raped."

Indeed, much of what people perceive as bad or dangerous about prostitution has to do with the fact that it is illegal. Sex workers have little protection when clients are violent or abusive, and they have no recourse from police officers who coerce them into providing free sex (in exchange for not being arrested). Research shows that decriminalizing or legalizing sex work actually reduces the spread of sexually transmitted diseases. In the Netherlands, where prostitution has been legal since 2000 and decriminalized since the 1970s, the spread of HIV is the lowest in the developed world.

Legalizing prostitution also reduces violence against women and cuts down on the trafficking of illegal immigrants and children. In fact, a major study done seven years after prostitution was legalized in the Netherlands found the number of illegal migrants working in the sex trade there had decreased, as had the number of under-age workers.

"Business owners keep a close eye on whether prostitutes have the required documents," concluded A. L. Daalder, lead author of the 2007 study. The researchers found no evidence of under-age prostitution in the non-licensed sector and "only rarely found" minors in licensed brothels.

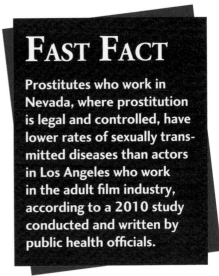

FAST FACT

Prostitutes who work in Nevada, where prostitution is legal and controlled, have lower rates of sexually transmitted diseases than actors in Los Angeles who work in the adult film industry, according to a 2010 study conducted and written by public health officials.

In the Netherlands, prostitutes work with law enforcement to target violent predators and traffickers. Decriminalizing or legalizing adult prostitution in the U.S. would allow law enforcement to focus their efforts on violent crime and on apprehending pimps who traffic in teenage runaways and illegal immigrants.

Offenses Committed Against Juvenile Victims in Prostitution Incidents

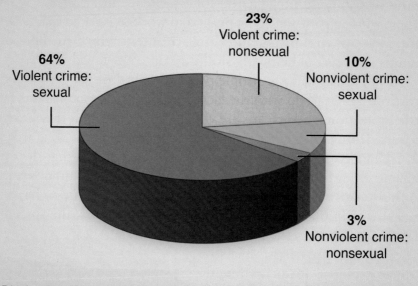

23%
Violent crime:
nonsexual

64%
Violent crime:
sexual

10%
Nonviolent crime:
sexual

3%
Nonviolent crime:
nonsexual

Taken from: Federal Bureau of Investigation, 1997–2000. National Criminal Justice Reference Service. "Prostitution of Juveniles: Patterns from NIBRS," June 2004.

Legalization Provides Prostitutes with New Channels for Help

The Canadian federal appeals court has already moved in this direction. In its landmark ruling in March, it amended the law against pimping to target only those who live off of prostitution "in circumstances of exploitation." In other words, sex workers in Ontario can hire pimps to protect them as long as there is no evidence that the pimps have coerced the women into the sex trade or are exploiting them.

The Canadian research also found an excessive use of force by police in enforcing laws against prostitution, making sex workers afraid of going to the police to report crimes. Contrast that with what happened in Cartagena, Colombia, where prostitution is legal: When a [US] Secret Service agent refused to pay a prostitute what he had promised her, the woman was able to summon a local police officer who took her side. That would never have happened in the United States.

Criminalizing prostitution also makes it difficult for addicted street walkers to access drug treatment, the Canadian study found. Since drug addiction increases the spread of sexually transmitted diseases, making prostitution legal and providing sex workers with access to health care and safe supportive housing could reduce the spread of HIV and other diseases, the British Columbia researchers said.

They concluded that Canada still has a long way to go toward providing the kind of housing and public health services that could reduce sexually transmitted diseases and violence against sex workers. But when it comes to changing archaic and regressive laws against prostitution, our northern neighbor is light years ahead of us.

EVALUATING THE AUTHOR'S ARGUMENTS:

After reading Alison Bass's viewpoint, do you think legalizing prostitution in the United States would have similar results as legalization of prostitution in the Netherlands? Or do you think that legalizing prostitution would cause a rise in STDs in America? Are there differences between the two countries that would cause the outcome to be different? If so, what are they? If not, why?

Legalizing and Regulating Prostitution Would Increase the Spread of STDs

"Enforcement of licensing and STI testing actually . . . increases STI rates."

Marina Adshade

In the viewpoint that follows Marina Adshade argues that legalizing prostitution will not have the intended result of making sex workers safer and reducing the spread of sexually transmitted diseases (STDs) but will instead help spread STDs. She contends that legalizing prostitution will create more sex workers, and many will not be able to get jobs in the "safe" indoor brothels and will have to work the streets, which will increase the number of sex workers on the street with STDs. Further, Adshade adds that regulating brothels will cause the cost of sex on the street to decrease, thus enticing men to take the risk of engaging in sex with a prostitute who is more likely to have an STD. It is this combination of factors that leads the author to conclude that regulating brothels will increase the incidence of STDs.

Marina Adshade, "Prostitution Paradox: Regulating Brothels Can Spread Disease," BigThink, August 10, 2010. Republished with permission.

Adshade is a Canadian blogger who posts on sex and politics on her blog *Dollars and Sex.*

AS YOU READ, CONSIDER THE FOLLOWING QUESTIONS:
1. According to the author, what will sex workers who cannot find a place in a brothel do?
2. The author argues that legalizing prostitution means it must be regulated, which drives up the price, which means what?
3. Adshade says that evidence from other countries with regulated brothels shows that enforcement of licensing and STD testing does what?

Prostitution, very narrowly defined, is not a criminal act in my country, Canada. If we are in a private home and I want to charge you for sex and no one is else profiting, the state has nothing to say on that.

Most acts of prostitution are, however, criminal acts. We have an ongoing national debate on the subject. Whenever this topic arises the argument is invariably that if prostitution is legalized, it can be regulated. That sounds like a good thing; taxes collected, STI's [sexually transmitted infections] controlled, minors taken off the street. I don't want to talk about morality or politics, now or ever, since *Dollars and Sex* [the author's blog] is blissfully free of such shackles. But I want to take a moment and ask the question: would legalization with regulation have the effect that we think it will?

FAST FACT

Two years after the Australian government legalized prostitution, studies showed that HIV infections in women increased by 91 percent.

Regulating Brothels Would Increase STI Risk on the Streets

Imagine we pass laws making it legal to run a brothel and that, in order to keep a license, condom use is enforced and workers need to

Opponents argue that legalizing prostitution will create more sex workers than can be safely managed and thus will increase STD rates.

be regularly tested for STI's. Presumably, this gets the workers off the streets and makes the selling of sex safer for everyone, including the spouses and partners of the clients. So far that sounds like it achieves some of society's objectives, right?

Let me ask you this: what happens to the sex trade worker who can't find a place in a brothel? Specifically, what about the worker who can't work in a brothel because she has an STI? In this regulated utopia, do these would-be sex-trade workers shrug their shoulders and apply for a job at [coffee-shop chain] Tim Hortons instead? Of course not. These workers are still out on the street, as are the minors and other workers who don't want to pay taxes. And what happens to the client who doesn't want to buy sex with a condom? Well those guys are not in the brothel either. They are out on the streets buying services from the most risky sellers, those who because of the regulations can't work in a brothel. Add to this the fact that regulations drive up brothel prices. So now, the street sector is comparatively cheaper, and many men are buying there regardless.

This isn't just speculation on my part. Evidence from countries with a regulated brothel sector shows that more enforcement of licensing and STI testing actually increases the number of sex trade workers on the streets. In addition, it increases STI rates and makes working in the sex trades more dangerous, not less. I suspect that those working in the sex trades in Canada know this, which is why the call is out for decriminalization, not legalization. No one in that sector is using the

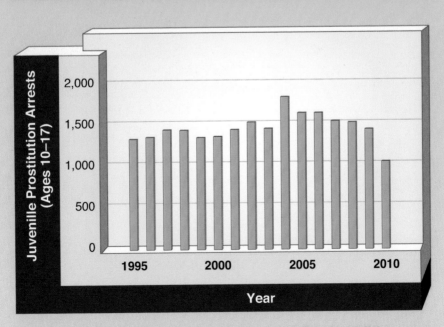

Taken from: Justitia Institute. "The 'Blue Campaign,' and Evidence on Human Trafficking," June 5, 2013.

regulation argument to justify a changing of the laws. If it is safety we are looking for, and if that means taking the sex trade off the streets, then regulation is not going to get us there.

Maybe we need to have a future conversation about who really benefits from decriminalization.

EVALUATING THE AUTHOR'S ARGUMENTS:

After reading this viewpoint by author Marina Adshade, do you think legalizing prostitution would lead to a rise in STDs? Or do you agree with the opposing viewpoint by Alison Bass that legalizing prostitution is a good way to deal with STDs? Use evidence from the viewpoints to support your claims.

Facts About Sexually Transmitted Diseases

Editor's note: These facts can be used in reports to add credibility when making important points or claims.

Prevalence and Cost
According to the Centers for Disease Control and Prevention (CDC):

- There are nearly 20 million new cases of sexually transmitted diseases [STDs] diagnosed each year in America.
- Half of these new infections occur in young people aged fifteen to twenty-four.
- Half of all people in the United States will acquire an STD before age twenty-five.
- The total number of people in the United States infected with an STD is approximately 110 million.
- STDs burden the health care system with $16 billion per year in direct costs. The lifelong diseases require the most health care dollars, but the curable diseases still cost the system $742 million each year.

Facts on the Eight Most Common STDs:
Chlamydia
- There are 2.86 million new cases in the United States each year.
- There are 1.57 million total cases in the United States.
- It can be treated and cured if diagnosed early.

Gonorrhea
- There are 820,000 new cases in the United States each year.
- About 570,000 of those 820,000 new cases annually involve young people fifteen to twenty-four years old.
- It can be treated and cured if diagnosed early.

Hepatitis B virus (HBV)
- There are 19,000 new cases in the United States each year.
- There are 422,000 total cases in the United States.
- There is no known cure.

Herpes simplex virus type 2 (HSV-2)
- There are 776,000 new cases in the United States each year.
- There are 24.1 million total cases in the United States.
- There is no known cure.

Human immunodeficiency virus (HIV)
- There are 41,400 new cases in the United States each year.
- As of 2011 an estimated 1,155,792 people in the United States have been diagnosed with AIDS, the disease caused by HIV.
- There is no known cure.

Human papillomavirus (HPV)
- There are 14.1 million new cases in the United States each year.
- There are 79.1 million total cases in the United States.
- Most HPV infections go away within two years after infection; about 10 percent can lead to serious health problems, such as cervical cancer.

Syphilis
- There are 55,400 new cases in the United States each year.
- Of the syphilis cases reported in 2012, 15,667 were of primary and secondary syphilis, the earliest and most transmissible stages of the disease.
- It can be treated and cured if diagnosed early.

Trichomoniasis
- There are 1.09 million new cases in the United States each year.
- There are 3.71 million total cases in the United States.
- It can be treated and cured if diagnosed early.

Detection and Health Care Responses

The Guttmacher Institute points out that because the symptoms of some STDs are difficult to observe without medical testing, infection rates may be higher than current estimates.

According to the *American Journal of Public Health*, less than one-third of physicians routinely screen patients for STDs.

According to the American Sexual Health Association (ASHA), less than half of adults aged eighteen to forty-four have ever been screened for an STD other than HIV/AIDS.

ASHA asserts that of the STDs/STIs that are diagnosed, only some (gonorrhea, syphilis, chlamydia, hepatitis A and B) are required to be reported to state health departments and the CDC.

Although it is time consuming and expensive, medical authorities rely on partner notification (that is, tracing and contacting persons known to have had sexual contact with an individual diagnosed with an STD) to help prevent the spread of these diseases.

Prevention

Citing several studies, ASHA reports that "consistent condom use provides substantial protection against the acquisition of many STDs, including statistically significant reduction of risk against HIV, chlamydia, gonorrhea, herpes, and syphilis."

The CDC states that routine condom use, abstinence, and fewer sexual partners are viable methods of reducing the spread of sexually transmitted infections.

Vaccines to prevent HPV and HBV are available. The HBV vaccine is routinely administered to newborns. The CDC recommends that the HPV vaccine be administered to children around age eleven or twelve.

According to the Mayo Clinic, male circumcision can reduce infection from HIV and certain types of HPV.

Organizations to Contact

The editors have compiled the following list of organizations concerned with the issues debated in this book. The descriptions are derived from materials provided by the organizations. All have publications or information available for interested readers. The list was compiled on the date of publication of the present volume; the information provided here may change. Be aware that many organizations take several weeks or longer to respond to inquiries, so allow as much time as possible for the receipt of requested materials.

Advocates for Youth
200 M St. NW, Ste. 750
Washington, DC 20036
(202) 419-3420 • fax: (202) 419-1448
website: www.advocatesforyouth.org

Advocates for Youth is an organization that seeks to help youth in America make personal decisions about their reproductive health based on the most current and accurate information available. The organization believes in promoting the core values of rights, respect, and responsibility (the three R's) in providing this information and entrusting youths to make their own decisions. The topics and issues covered by the organization are broad and include abstinence, condom efficacy and use, and sexually transmitted infections among many others. Detailed information and reports about these topics can be found on its website.

American Sexually Transmitted Disease Association (ASTDA)
PO Box 12665, Research Triangle Park
NC 27709
(919) 861-9399
e-mail: astda@astda.org
website: www.astda.org

ASTDA is dedicated to supporting research on and developing ways to control, prevent, and ultimately eradicate STDs. In addition to these activities, the organization also publishes educational information about STDs. ASTDA provides access to a range of resources, including the 2010 *STD Treatment Guidelines* published by the Centers for Disease Control and Prevention, the World Health Organization Sexually Transmitted Diseases Diagnostics Initiative, and the Online STD Case Series. *Sexually Transmitted Diseases* is the official journal of the organization, publishing peer-reviewed articles on STD research.

AVERT HIV/AIDS

4 Brighton Rd., Horsham
West Sussex, RH13 5BA, UK
+44 (0)1403 210 202
e-mail: info@avert.org
website: www.avert.org

AVERT is an international HIV/AIDS charity dedicated to finding ways to stop the spread of the disease through treatment and prevention, providing information about the disease to the public, researching developments related to the disease, and advocating on behalf of individuals with the disease. Detailed information about a variety of topics—including HIV prevention, transmission, testing, treatment, and care; living with HIV; and HIV's impact on young people—can all be found on the AVERT website.

Centers for Disease Control and Prevention (CDC)

1600 Clifton Rd.
Atlanta, GA 30333
(800) 232-4636
website: www.cdc.gov

The CDC is the national agency in the United States charged with ensuring that the health of the nation's citizens is protected and with preventing and controlling disease, injury, and disability. Through its educational and research programs, the CDC works to educate the public about measures people can take to improve and protect their own health and to develop government policies and strategies to help US citizens live better lives. The Division of STD Prevention (DSTDP) within the CDC is specifically tasked with leading national efforts to prevent and control STDs, developing policy on this topic, and working with outside organizations on these efforts. Extensive information about STDs can be found on the DSTDP website, including diseases and related conditions, prevention, publication and products, and data and statistics.

Henry J. Kaiser Family Foundation
2400 Sand Hill Rd.
Menlo Park, CA 94025
(650) 854-9400 • fax: (650) 854-4800
website: www.kff.org

The Henry J. Kaiser Family Foundation is a nonprofit, private operating organization dedicated to addressing the major US health care issues. Through its in-house research and its journalism and communications programs, Kaiser seeks to provide a reliable voice and source of information for policy makers, the media, health care professionals, and the public. While the organization's topics of focus span all areas of health and wellness, it has focused efforts on HIV/AIDS prevention and awareness around the world. The Kaiser website about the disease provides current information about the impact of health policy on HIV/AIDS treatment, statistics about infection rates, and current research.

Office of Adolescent Health (OAH)
1101 Wootton Pkwy., Ste. 700, Rockville, MD 20852
e-mail: oah.gov@hhs.gov
website: www.hhs.gov/ash/oah

OAH is an office within the US Department of Health and Human Services charged with finding ways to ensure that adolescents in the United States enjoy high standards of health and have the opportunity to grow into healthy and productive adults. Recently, efforts of the OAH have focused on the reproductive health of youth. Within this topic, issues such as STDs and contraceptive and condom use receive individual attention. Extensive statistics on STD infection rates among US teens and their use of a variety of contraception options can be found on the OAH website. Additionally, OAH online offers visitors a range of more-detailed publications on these topics.

Planned Parenthood Federation of America
434 W. Thirty-Third St.
New York, NY 10001

(212) 541-7800 • fax: (212) 245-1845
website: www.plannedparenthood.org

Planned Parenthood is a national reproductive health care, education, and advocacy organization that has been providing services to women and men in the United States for nearly a century through its seventy-one locally governed affiliates around the nation and close to 750 health centers. Most of the care it provides focuses on preventative measures to decrease the incidence of unwanted pregnancy using contraception, halt the spread of STDs, and scan for cervical and other forms of cancer. Educational resources about STD-related topics can be accessed on the Planned Parenthood website and include issues such as safer sex, STD testing, and information about specific diseases.

Population Council
One Dag Hammarskjöld Plaza, 9th Fl.
New York, NY 10017
(212) 339-0500; toll-free: (877) 339-0500 • fax: (212) 755-6052
website: www.popcouncil.org

The Population Council is an international organization that works to conduct research on biomedicine, social science, and public health, with the intent of helping governments and organizations worldwide to shape public policy, programs, and technology in order to help all the world's people improve their lives. One of the main areas of focus is HIV and AIDS, particularly increasing knowledge of the disease's spread and finding ways to stop it. Resources on this disease available on the organization's website include fact sheets about the program and at-risk populations, along with detailed reports on Population Council projects on HIV/AIDS from around the world.

Sexuality Information and Education Council of the United States (SIECUS)
90 John St., Ste. 402
New York, NY 10038
(212) 819-9770 • fax: (212) 819-9776
website: www.siecus.org

SIECUS is an organization that has been working since its founding in 1964 to educate the public—particularly schools and parents—about sex and sexuality, to advocate for good sex education policies, and to inform everyone about sex-related issues, using the most current research and resources on these topics. The organization's website provides comprehensive information on a range of issues, including different sex-education approaches, adolescent sexuality, and STDs among others. Fact sheets, publications, bibliographies, and additional resources for these and other topics can be found online.

World Health Organization (WHO)
Avenue Appia 20
1211 Geneva 27
Switzerland
+ 41 22 791 21 11 • fax: + 41 22 791 31 11
website: www.who.int

WHO is an international organization that works within the United Nations to address all health-related issues and topics. Its focuses include leading international global health efforts, defining what health research will be conducted, establishing norms and standards, developing policy recommendations based on solid evidence, assisting countries with their health programs, and observing world health trends. One topic among the many addressed by the WHO is sexually transmitted infections, and information online includes general information fact sheets, technical information, regional information, publications, and a link to the WHO Department of Reproductive Health and Research.

For Further Reading

Books

Grimes, Jill A. *Seductive Delusions: How Everyday People Catch STDs.* Baltimore: Johns Hopkins University Press, 2008. The author, a medical doctor, uses personal stories and facts to convince readers that STDs are prevalent throughout society and not limited to specific groups or classes of people.

Grodek, Brett. *The First Year: HIV; An Essential Guide for the Newly Diagnosed.* 2nd ed. New York: Marlowe, 2007. An HIV-positive patient relates practical information about living with the infection and the support networks and lifestyle choices available to those diagnosed with HIV.

Handsfield, H. Hunter. *Color Atlas & Synopsis of Sexually Transmitted Diseases.* 3rd ed. New York: McGraw-Hill, 2011. This overview contains informative text and images that describe numerous STDs, as well as their treatment and prevention.

Marr, Lisa. *Sexually Transmitted Diseases: A Physician Tells You What You Need to Know.* Baltimore: Johns Hopkins University Press, 2007. A doctor provides basic information on sexually transmitted diseases and their prevention, diagnosis, and treatment.

Nack, Adina. *Damaged Goods? Women Living with Incurable Sexually Transmitted Diseases.* Philadelphia: Temple University Press, 2008. This book contains a frank series of interviews with women living with herpes or HPV who discuss their sexual identities and means of control given the incurable status of their diseases.

Stanberry, Lawrence R. *Understanding Herpes.* 2nd ed. Jackson: University Press of Mississippi, 2006. The author notes recent methods of diagnosing and treating one of the most common STDs, including information on the use of antiviral therapy and the connection between herpes and the risk of HIV infection.

Tenney, Louise. *Herpes: A Nutritional Approach.* Salt Lake City: Woodland, 1996. After providing a description of this common

STD, the author lists various vitamins and herbal agents that supposedly boost the immune system and reduce the irritation associated with herpes.

Whiteside, Alan. *HIV/AIDS: A Very Short Introduction.* New York: Oxford University Press, 2008. This is an admittedly brief overview of the disease that includes a look at its history and demographic realities in order to suggest a remedial response.

Yancey, Diane. *STDs: What You Don't Know Can Hurt You.* Minneapolis: Twenty-First Century, 2002. A book aimed at young readers, this volume gives a general overview of many common STDs and the means of their prevention and treatment.

Periodicals

Baar, Karen. "Worth the Wait," *Human Sexuality Supplement,* October 2007.

Daly, Melissa. "No Glove, No Love," *Human Sexuality Newsletter,* November 2011.

Giacobbe, Alyssa. "The New Sex Cancer," *Men's Health,* September 2011.

Goodwine, Nina. "1 Flesh: Putting the 'Sexy' Back in Abstinence," *Humanist,* September/October 2012.

Groopman, Jerome. "Sex and the Superbug," *New Yorker,* October 1, 2012.

Grumman, Rachel. "How to Outsmart STDs," *Cosmopolitan,* October 2010.

Gulati, Richa. "Risky Business," *Teen Vogue,* December 2012.

Hawkins, B. Denise. "Thirty Years Later: AIDS Experts Reflect on Efforts to Eradicate the Disease, Create Awareness About How It Is Transmitted," *Diverse: Issues in Higher Education,* September 2011.

Healy, Bernadine. "Clueless About Risks of Oral Sex," *U.S. News & World Report,* March 10, 2008.

Herper, Matthew. "The Gardasil Problem," *Forbes,* April 23, 2012.

Hirshberg, Charles. "Should All Males Be Circumcised?," *Men's Health,* March 2009.

Jacobson, Malia, and Caitlin Carlson. "Would You Bleep Someone with an STD?," *Women's Health*, July/August 2012.

Kantor, Leslie M. "Abstinence-Only Education Violating Students' Rights to Health Information," *Human Rights*, Summer 2008.

Krakauer, Hannah. "See Ya, Latex!," *New Scientist*, January 19, 2013.

McKenna, Maryn. "Return of the Clap," *Scientific American*, May 2012.

Melby, Todd. "Obama Delivers, Mostly," *Contemporary Sexuality*, June 2010.

Powell, Tracie. "Black Woman's Burden," *Crisis*, Summer 2009.

Williamsen, Kurt. "The High Cost of 'Hooking Up,'" *New American*, January 7, 2013.

Websites

Advocates for Youth (www.advocatesforyouth.org). Advocates for Youth is a grassroots organization that provides information to young people concerning sexual health and family planning. It stresses the three R's (rights, respect, and responsibility) in helping individuals make decisions about their sexual well-being. The organization's website contains videos and written resources concerning STDs and other pertinent concerns.

American Sexually Transmitted Diseases Association (www.astda .org). A support and education organization, ASTDA brings together researchers to study STDs in the hope of eradicating these diseases. The organization's website has an assortment of information for members, but nonmembers can follow links to government documents and other materials helpful in understanding STDs and attendant policies.

American Social Health Association (www.ashastd.org). A venerable public institution, ASHA collates the most up-to-date information and statistics on STDs and provides fact sheets and other documents to educators, policy makers, and interested individuals. The goal of ASHA is to keep discussion of STDs prominent as a way of reducing them and their terrible social costs.

CDC National Center for HIV/AIDS, Viral Hepatitis, STD, and TB Prevention (www.cdc.gov/nchhstp). The Centers for Disease Control and Prevention's (CDC's) basic information site compiles statistics and data from government research into all these illnesses. The website presents general information on the named diseases and houses yearly surveillance reports that track the spread of each disease and efforts to curb infection rates.

CDC National Prevention Information Network (www.cdcnpin .org). Part of the CDC, the network serves as a clearinghouse for material related to HIV/AIDS and other STDs. Information can be gleaned from documents created on national, state, and local levels. The site also provides referral service to those seeking more help.

National Chlamydia Coalition (http://ncc.prevent.org). Founded in 2008, the National Chlamydia Coalition (NCC) is a collection of health advocates, insurers, and politicians who are determined to educate young people about the dangers of contracting chlamydia. The organization's website offers information and products to help increase awareness of the disease.

National Institute of Allergy and Infectious Diseases (www.niaid .nih.gov). Part of the National Institutes of Health, this government organization provides newsletters and Internet forums relating to technological breakthroughs and the science involved in combating STDs and other infectious diseases.

Project Inform (www.projectinform.org). The intent of Project Inform is to ensure that individuals living with HIV are represented in the care and treatment responses to the disease. Its policy is to give HIV-positive persons a voice in the fight against AIDS and to help better the health of those infected with HIV. The website contains "HIV Health & Wellness" booklets that are available, along with other information.

Index

numbers diagnosed/reported *vs.* estimated totals, *91*

prevalence of new infections, by age group, *45*

Cochrane Collaboration, 52

Community Based Abstinence Education (CBAE), 50–51

Comprehensive sex education

helps prevent spread of STDs, 49–56

increase in federal funding for, 66

Condoms, 9, 72

value of abstinence and, 68–74

Contraception, *85*

D

Daalder, A. L., 105

Department of Health and Human Services, US, 58, 66, 71

DeVries, Brian, 85

The Dignity of Restraint (Bhikkhu), 72–74

Dittrich, Boris, 28

Downing, Nancy, 22, 27–28

Dwyer, Kathleen, 10

F

Families United to Prevent Teen Pregnancy program, 65–66

Fineberg, Harvey V., 49

Five Years of Abstinence-Only-Until-Marriage Education (Hauser), 82

For Keeps curriculum, 63–64

Fortner, Tye, 20–22, 24–25, 26, 28–29

Freedman, Rosa, 88

G

Gay and Lesbian Alliance Against Defamation (GLAAD), 15

Genital herpes. *See* Herpes simplex

Giuliani, Rudy, 28

GLAAD (Gay and Lesbian Alliance Against Defamation), 15

Gonorrhea, 33

means of infection, 8

numbers diagnosed/reported *vs.* estimated totals, *91*

prevalence of new infections, by age group, *45*

Government, should mandate HPV vaccine, 98–102

Granuloma inguinale, means of infection, 8

Grossberg, Robert, 22

Guaylupo, Johnny, 25

Guttmacher Institute, 100

H

HASA (HIV/AIDS Services Administration, New York City), 22–23

Hauser, Debra, 82–84, 85

Hepatitis B, 52

means of transmission, 8

Heritage Keepers program, 63, 70–72

Herpes simplex, *95,* 95–96

means of transmission, 8

new infections, prevalence by age group, *45*

prevalence of, 8–9

High school dropout rates, among sexually active *vs.* abstinent teens, *71*

HIV (human immunodeficiency virus), 8

homeless may intentionally become infected with, 19–29

infection rates, prostitution and, 105, 109

new infections among men age 13–24, *23*

new infections of, *16*

percentage of infections among teens, 24

percentage of US population infected with, 9

removing stigma attached to, would
reduce, 93–97
risk of contracting, increases with
pubic hair removal, 41–47
spread of among senior citizens,
36–40
virginity pledges do not reduce
spread of, 80–86
See also specific diseases
Shannon, Kate, 105
Sharifi, Maral Noshad, 19
Social Science and Medicine (journal),
104
Staley, Peter, 12
State Abstinence Education Program,
50
Surveys
on impact of abstinence programs,
65, 84
of parents, on importance of
abstinence-only education, 62
Syphilis
means of infection, 8
prevalence of new infections, by age
group, *45*

T
Talbot, Margaret, 86
Teenagers
abstinence behavior among, *64*
numbers receiving sex education,
by topic/gender, *54*
percentage of HIV infections
among, 24
prevalence of sexual activity among,
58
sexually active *vs.* abstinent, high
school dropout rates among,
71

taking virginity pledges,
contraception use among, *vs.*
non-pledgers, *85*
use of condoms and STD
prevalence among, 72
virginity pledges work for some,
75–79
Teens in Control program, 65–66
Title V (Social Security Act), 82–83
Treatment, for HIV, adherence rates
for, 14
Trichomoniasis, means of
transmission, 8
Truvada, 9

U
United States, Windsor v. (2013), *13*
University of Maryland School of
Public Health, 33

V
Vaid, Urvashi, 16
Virginity pledges
contraception use among teens
taking, *vs.* non-pledgers, *85*
do not reduce spread of STDs,
80–86
work for some teens, 75–79

W
Weber, Mark, 70
Weinstein, Michael, 9
Windsor v. United States (2013), *13*
Women
binge drinking increases STD risk
among, 30–35
older, lack of HPV screening
among, 38–40
prevalence of high- *vs.* low-risk
HPV among, *101*

Picture Credits

© AP Images/Matt Rourke, 73

© AP Images/Reed Saxon, 51

© Cengage/Gale, 16, 23, 32, 45, 54, 64, 71, 78, 85, 91, 101, 106, 111

© Cultura RM/Alamy, 39

© Directphoto.org/Alamy, 15

© images-USA/Alamy, 90

© Ted Jackson/The Times-Picayune/Landov, 27

© jvphoto/Alamy, 34

© Marvl Lacar/Getty Images, 77

© Medical-on-Line/Alamy, 43, 95

© Ian Nolan/Alamy, 87

© Radharc Images/Alamy, 48

© Joe Raedle/Getty Images, 99

© Dibyangshu Sarkar/AFP/Getty Images, 61

© Stocktrek Images, Inc./Alamy, 11

© David White/Alamy, 110